山东省齐文化研究基地重点项目
Major Project of Shandong Provincial Research Base on Kingdom Qi's Culture
山东省齐文化传承与示范区建设协同创新中心重点项目
Key Project of Collaborative Innovation Center of Shandong Provincial Inheritance & Demonstration Construction
on Kingdom Qi's Culture
山东理工大学齐文化研究院重点项目
Key Program of Kingdom Qi's Culture Academy of Shandong University of Technology

管子生平传略图谱

王京龙 文　郭振华 绘　夏晓慧 译

中国海洋大学出版社
·青岛·

图书在版编目（CIP）数据

管子生平传略图谱 / 王京龙文；郭振华绘；夏晓慧译. —青岛：中国海洋大学出版社，2020.11
ISBN 978−7−5670−2691−9

Ⅰ.①管… Ⅱ.①王… ②郭… ③夏… Ⅲ.①管仲（？—前645）—生平事迹—图谱 Ⅳ.①B226.1−64

中国版本图书馆CIP数据核字（2020）第246705号

管子生平传略图谱

出版发行	中国海洋大学出版社		
社　　址	青岛市香港东路23号	邮政编码	266071
出 版 人	杨立敏		
网　　址	http://pub.ouc.edu.cn		
电子邮箱	184385208@qq.com		
订购电话	0532−82032573（传真）		
责任编辑	付绍瑜	电　　话	0532−85902533
印　　制	淄博华义印刷有限公司		
版　　次	2020年12月第1版		
印　　次	2020年12月第1次印刷		
成品尺寸	185 mm × 260 mm		
印　　张	9.5		
字　　数	137千		
印　　数	1～1000		
定　　价	59.00元		

发现印装质量问题，请致电0533−2782115，由印刷厂负责调换。

　　王京龙（1959—2019），山东淄博人，山东理工大学齐文化研究院教授，山东省齐文化研究基地首席专家，享受山东理工大学高层次人才（二层次）特殊津贴，主要从事齐文化与中国传统文化的研究和教学工作。

　　其出版著作有《战国百家争鸣与中华传统体育精神构架》（人民出版社）、《管子与孔子的历史对话》（齐鲁书社）、《管子通论》（齐鲁书社）、《齐国人本思想研究》（山东人民出版社）、《齐国威宣盛世》（山东文艺出版社）、《齐文化与中国古代体育》（齐鲁书社）、《齐文化旅游概论》（山东人民出版社）、《齐文化旅游丛书》（中华书局）等；在《体育科学》《社会科学战线》《北京体育大学学报》《体育科学》《齐鲁学刊》等期刊发表论文60余篇，有多篇被中国人民大学复印报刊资料、《新华文摘》、《文摘报》等报刊转载；主持完成国家社科基金课题、省部级课题10余项。

Professor Wang Jinglong (1959−2019) was from Zibo City, Shandong Province. He was a professor of Kingdom Qi's Culture Academy of Shandong University of Technology (SDUT), a master tutor and chief expert of Shandong Provincial Research Base on Kingdom Qi's Culture who enjoyed a special allowance for high-level talents (second level) of SDUT, mainly engaged in the

作者简介

郭振华／绘

簡子博略園譜

管子生平传略图谱

王京龙／文
夏晓慧／译

research and teaching of Kingdom Qi's Culture and Chinese traditional culture.

His published works includes *The Controversy of the Hundred Schools of the Warring States Period and the Traditional Chinese Sports Spiritual Framework* (People's Publishing House), *The Historical Dialogue Between Master Guan Zhong and Confucius* (Qilu Press), *The General Theory of Master Guan Zhong* (Qilu Press), *Research on Kingdom Qi's Humanistic Thought* (Shandong People's Publishing House), *Kingdom Qi's Heyday During Kings Wei & King Xuan Regime* (Shandong Literature & Art Publishing House), *Kingdom Qi's Culture and Ancient Chinese Sports* (Qilu Press), *An Introduction to Kingdom Qi's Culture Tourism Outline* (Shandong People's Publishing House), *Kingdom Qi's Culture Tourism Series* (Zhonghua Book Co.) and others. So far, more than 60 papers in journals such as *China Sports Science*, *Social Science Front*, *Journal of Beijing Sport University*, *Sports Science*, *Qilu Journal* were published, many of which were reproduced by *Reproduced Journals of Renmin University of China*, *Xinhua Digest*, *Digest News* and other newspapers and periodicals. Besides, he presided and completed more than 10 national social science fund projects and provincial and ministerial projects.

郭振华，山东淄博人，书画家，中国书协会员，舒同书法研究会（全国）副会长兼山东舒同书画研究院副理事长，中国楹联学会会员兼书艺委委员，中国水墨艺术研究院艺委会委员，山东理工大学兼职教授。出版著作有《怎样搞好店容店貌》（山东人民出版社）、《天下第一村：周村》（山东友谊书社）、《郭振华书舒体真草千字文》（山东人民出版社），主编《舒同百年纪念文集》（中国文史出版社）、《管子与孔子的历史对话》（插图绘制，齐鲁书社）。

Professor Guo Zhenhua, from Zibo, Shandong Province is a calligrapher and painter, a member of the Chinese Calligraphy Association, the vice president of the Shutong Calligraphy Research Association (nationwide) and vice chairman of the Shandong Shutong Calligraphy & Painting Research Institute, a member of the Chinese Society of Couplets and a member of the Calligraphy & Arts Committee, a member of Art Committee of China Ink Art Research Institute and a part-time professor of Shandong University of Technology (SDUT). His published books include *How to Improve the Appearance of Your Store* (Shandong People's Publishing House), *The First Village Under the Sun: Zhoucun Village* (Shandong Friendship Publishing House), *Guo Zhenhua's Shutong Style Cursive Script Thousand Characters* (Shandong People's Publishing House), *Shutong Centennial Anniversary Collection* (editor-in-chief) (China Literature and History Press), *Historical Dialogue Between Master Guan Zhong and Confucius* (illustrator) (Qilu Press).

作者简介

郭振华／绘

夏晓慧，陕西咸阳人，武汉大学信息管理学院管理学硕士，现为山东理工大学科技信息研究所副研究馆员、中国科技翻译工作者协会注册会员、中国科协自然科学专门学会会员、中国图书馆学会会员与山东省图书馆学会会员，主要从事科技翻译与参考咨询的研究与教学工作。在《中国科技翻译》《情报资料工作》《情报杂志》与《现代情报》等刊物发表论文、译文70余篇，译著1部，合著5部，主持完成教育部项目1项；参与国家、省部级与厅局级项目10余项；获得各级各类奖励10余项。

Xia Xiaohui, from Xianyang, Shaanxi Province, with the master degree of management, School of Information Management, Wuhan University, is currently an associate research librarian at the Institute of Science and Technology Information, Shandong University of Technology (SDUT) and mainly engages in research of translation of science and technology and reference consulting and teaching. She is a registered member of the Chinese Translators Association of Science and Technology, a member of the Chinese Academy of Science and Technology Specialized Society, a member of the Chinese Library Society and the Shandong Provincial Library Association. She published more than 70 papers and translations in journals including *Chinese Science & Technology Translators Journal*, *Information and Documentation Services*, *Journal of Intelligence* and *Journal of Modern Information*, 1 translated book, 5 books co-edited and participated and won awards in more than 10 national, provincial, ministerial, and departmental level projects.

简子生平传略图谱

管子生平传略图谱

王京龙／文
夏晓慧／译

序

　　由王京龙教授策划、撰文，郭振华绘图，夏晓慧英译的《管子生平传略图谱》即将出版，这是一本展示齐文化面貌，传承、弘扬齐文化精神的有创意的著作，很值得祝贺！

　　齐文化博大精深，为中华文明贡献至伟。如果历数一下其中的大事件，管仲辅佐齐桓称霸是最突出的重大事件之一。因此，司马迁作《史记》，为宰相立传，管仲为第一人，与晏婴合传。后世称赞管仲是中国历史上最伟大的政治家。记载管仲事迹、思想的《管子》一书，被称为中国早期政治智慧集大成的经典著作。该书以管仲为主体创作，抓住了弘扬齐文化的关键人物和重大事件，意义自在其中。

　　中国文化史上，往往将人格最高尚、智慧最卓绝的人，称为"圣人"。例如，孟子说"尧、舜既殁，圣人之道衰"，即是将尧、舜看作圣人的。孔子在众多圣人之中，被历代统治者尊奉、加封为"至圣"。今人则常把历史上某个领域中，第一个贡献最大、成就最突出的人物冠以"圣人"之名，如"医圣""书圣"。我们将历史上第一个治国理政业绩最突出的伟大政治家管仲称为"圣人"，是完全可以的。圣人而有"圣迹图"传世的是孔子。明代即有《孔子圣迹图》的创制，后经历代学者的补充、修改、完善，形成石刻、印制版传世至今。近些年来，有的学者和艺术家也仿照《孔子圣迹图》先后创制了伏羲、老子、孟子等的"圣迹图"，对弘扬中国优秀传统文化起了有力推动。现在，《管子生平传略图谱》的问世，是对弘扬管子优秀文化传统的一个创新性贡献。

　　王京龙教授是一位将终生精力和志趣都投入齐文化研究中的学者。他在担任山东理工大学齐文化研究院教授、山东省齐文化研究基地首席专家

郭振华／绘

的若干年中，为人正派，治学勤奋，成果丰硕，为推动齐文化研究和传播作出了突出贡献。不幸积劳成疾，于2019年英年早逝。本书稿其生前已经完成，今由其夫人宁秀红女士参与，与郭振华、夏晓慧等同志一起进行了整理，由山东理工大学齐文化研究院支持资助出版，这既圆满实现了一项有价值成果的问世，也是对京龙教授最好的纪念。是为序。

王志民
2020年6月26日于山东理工大学

EXORDIUM

First let us congratulate the publication of this *Master Guan Zhong's Lifetime Pictures Story*. The initiator and writer of this book is Prof. Wang Jinglong, with Prof. Guo Zhenhua as the illustrator and Ms. Xia Xiaohui as the English version translator. This novelty book is to show the characteristics of Kingdom Qi's Culture, to inherit and advance and enrich its great thinking from generation to generation.

Kingdom Qi's Culture is broad in scope and profound in effect, and is one of the greatest contributors to the Chinese civilization. Among those outstanding personages and their highlighted contributions in history, the most prominent event must be prime minister Guan Zhong helped Duke Huan of Qi transform Kingdom Qi into China's most powerful polity. A great historian of Han Dynasty, named Sima Qian, wrote a biography for a prime minister Guan Zhong, it was the first of its kind in history. This biography also contained the life story of Yan Ying, another noted prime minister of a later generation in the kingdom. This duo-biography was just in the *Records of the Grand Historian*, a monumental history of ancient China and the world. Later generations praise Guan Zhong as the greatest statesman in Chinese history. A book called *Guan Zi* well recorded his noted achievements and wisdom thinking, and is the classic of early Chinese political wisdom.

In the long history of Chinese culture, those people with the most noble personality and most outstanding wisdom are usually regarded as "sages". For example, philosopher Mencius once said: "When Emperors Yao and Shun died, Tao of sages also declined." Yao and Shun were wise monarchs with

序

序

郭振华／绘

3

both virtue and talent in ancient history. That is to say, Yao and Shun were worshiped as sages. Confucius was the only one often worshiped and ennobled as sacrosanctity by rulers at different dynasties. Later offspring would crown with the title sage to a historical figure who was the first person with the most contribution in a field, such as a medical sage, a caligraphy sage. Today it is entirely right and logical for us to honor Guan Zhong, the first great statesman with outstanding governance performance in history, as a "sage". People respectfully called him Guan Zi. This suffix "Zi" just means something as sage. Confucius is the first sage whose "sacred footprints" handed down from ancient times. The *Confucius Sacred Footprints Story* was created, first off, during the Ming Dynasty, and after being replenished, modified and perfected during successive dynasties, the stone carving version and printed version are handed down. In recent years, some scholars and artists have also created sacred footprints successively for the earliest Chinese legendary Emperor Fu Xi, for Lao Zi, the founder of Taoism, for great philosopher Mencius as well. They all based on the *Confucius Sacred Footprints Story*. All these work is a strong impetus to promote the excellent Chinese traditional culture. Now we have this crafting publication of *Master Guan Zhong's Lifetime Pictures Story*. It is a novelty contribution to develop and roll out Kingdom Qi's cultural heritage even worldwide.

Prof. Wang Jinglong is a scholars who devoted his lifetime energy and aspiration and interest to the study of Kingdom Qi's Culture. During his years as a professor of the Kingdom Qi's Cultural Academy (KQCA) of Shandong University of Technology (SDUT) and the chief expert of the Shandong Kingdom Qi Cultural Research Base (SKQCRB), he was decent in personal conduct and industrious in scholar work with fruitful researching results. Thus he made outstanding contributions to promoting the research and the popularization of Kingdom Qi's Culture. Unfortunately, due to his sleepless devotion, he suddenly died of illness at an early age in 2019. The Chinese manuscript of this book was already edited

管子生平传略图谱

王京龙／文
夏晓慧／译

4

and finished during his life time. Then his wife, Madam Ning Xiuhong, together with Prof. Guo Zhenhua and Ms. Xia Xiaohui, compiled his work. They got timely support with financial aid for the publication from KQCA of SDUT. A mutual closer cooperation among all these great people enabled this book to complete in time in front of us. This not only makes a valuable outcome published, but also is the best everlasting commemoration of Prof. Wang Jinglong.

Thus having this above as a preface.

Wang Zhimin at SDUT

June 26th, 2020

序

序

郭振华 / 绘

前 言

　　管仲（？—前645年），姬姓，管氏，名夷吾，字仲，又字敬仲。司马迁称其为"颍上人也"。中国历史上春秋时期的齐国国相，齐桓公尊称为仲父，著名的政治家。后人把他的思想理论和社会实践的汇集阐释辑录成为《管子》一书。因其事功而成其著述，因其著述而名垂千古，名扬海内外。孔子说："管仲相桓公，霸诸侯，一匡天下，民到于今受其赐。微管仲，吾其被发左衽矣。"意思是说，管仲辅佐齐桓公成就的霸业，其功德惠及后世。假如没有管仲的话，我们都要像落后地区的人们那样披散着头发，衣服的大襟向左边开着，袒胸露乳地生活在愚昧落后的时代。

　　概括管子一生的突出贡献，一是以"仓廪实则知礼节，衣食足则知荣辱"为目标，"贵轻重，慎权衡"，通过一系列的变革措施，让齐国富强起来，齐桓公成为诸侯霸主，开创了"不慕古，不留今，与时变，与俗化"变革发展的先河；二是高举"尊王攘夷"的旗帜，辅佐齐桓公"九合诸侯，一匡天下"，维护了华夏文明的延续与发展，形成了中华民族文化共同体的雏形；三是以《管子》一书为载体，为人类社会发展留下了一份弥足珍贵的精神财富。

　　梁启超说："今天下言治术者，有最要之名词数四焉：曰国家思想也，曰法治精神也，曰地方制度也，曰经济竞争也，曰帝国主义也。此数者皆近二三百年来之产物，新萌芽而新发达者，欧美人所以雄于天下者，曰惟有此之故。中国人所以弱于天下者，曰惟无此之故。中国人果无此乎？曰恶，是何言？吾见吾中国人之发达是而萌芽是，有更先于欧美者。

谓余不信，请语管子。"略管子其事功而读管子其论述，"经纬日月，用之于民"的博大胸怀，不仅在2600多年前"普天之下，莫非王土"的古代社会中难得一见，即便是今天民主制度不断进步的社会发展中，也是十分难能可贵的。

管子其人与《管子》其书，是人类社会历史上的瑰宝，崛起于中国临淄而走向全世界，伴随日月的轮转而熠熠生辉。中国有句古诗，叫作"高山仰止，景行行止。"管子其人与《管子》其书作为人类历史上不朽的丰碑，耸立于天地之间，镌刻着先贤的聪明和智慧，昭示着后人前进的方向。

有济、淮之水而有东夷文明，由东夷文明而孕育了齐鲁文化，巍巍乎，孔子是鲁文化的大大纛；浩浩乎，管子则是齐文化的星标。无孔子无以言及鲁文化和儒学，无管子则无以言及齐文化。

简子生平传略图谱

管子生平传略图谱

王京龙／文
夏晓慧／译

PREFACE

　　Guan Zhong (? —645BC), a descendant of Clan Ji. Guan is his family name. With given name Yiwu, he styled himself Zhong, also Jingzhong. So you can call him Guan Zhong, or in the western way Zhong Guan, also Guan Yiwu, Guan Jingzhong. People often call him Guan Zi, or Master Guan Zhong, as the honorific suffix Zi in classic Chinese refers to somebody respectful as a sage, or Master. Sima Qian, a great historian, said Guan Zhong was "a native of Yingshang". He was prime minister of State Qi during the Spring and Autumn Period. Duke Huan of Qi addressed him respectfully as Uncle Zhong. Later generations collected his theory and activities, then compiled a book with his respectful name *Guan Zi*. His contributions and achievements formed this work, which thus has an everlasting name for a long span of time and a brilliant reputation both at home and abroad. Confucius once said: "Guan Zhong, as the prime minister, assisted Duke Huan of Qi to become the first lord protector of all the feudal princes and set everything right throughout the state. Even up to the present day, the people are still enjoying the benefits he conferred. Without Guan Zhong, we would still be like the people in rude tribes, whose hair is unbound and the lappets of coats unbuttoned on the left side. Without Guan Zhong, we would have remained barbarian tribes and be ignorant and backward."

　　His achievements are summarized and highlighted as the following three points. The first contribution is enriching State Qi, by following the target of

前言

郭振华／绘

3

"man will observe the proprieties and obligations when his granary is full; man will have a sense of honor and humility when he has enough food and clothing". By attaching importance to order of priority, cautiously weighing the pros and cons, and through multiple reforms, he enriched the State Qi and made his lord Duke Huan the first and most powerful lord protector of all the feudal princes; by initiating the policy as "Do not worship the ancient ways nor be entrenched in your opinions; adjust yourself as the times and prevailing custom change." The second contribution is holding high the banner of "Honouring the King of Zhou Dynasty and driving off the barbarians". Through appointing Guan Zhong as his Prime Minister, Duke Huan became the first powerful leader of the feudal princes, uniting and reducing to good order all that is under Heaven; all these actions well preserve the continuation and development of Chinese civilization, and formed a rudiment of ethnic cultural community of Chinese; the third contribution is his precious spiritual wealth left behind him, with this works *Guan Zi*, or *Master Guan Zhong's Works*, for the whole development of human society.

Liang Qichao, a noted modern scholar commented: "there are 4 key nouns describing the present day popular different governance systems, namely nationalism, rule of law, local-oriented system, economic competition, and imperialism. They are just outcome of past two to three hundred years old, the reason that these European and American nations are powerful on earth is just because of these new outcome, a new bud develops new prosperous. China's weakness on the world is because we don't have such systems in China. Doesn't China sure enough have such in fact? Yes, why is that? I noted from history that China also developed such view well and it germinated, much earlier than those European and American nations. If you are not convinced, take Master Guan Zhong for example." Even not mention what Master Guan did and his contribution, just reading his works, his broad and profound mind. "To Master the operation law of the sun and the moon, to apply that spirit to your people in a way that is just and fair to all", this concept was rare in ancient society 2,600 years before, when all tract of land under the sun belongs to the king. Even today, his thought and concept is rare and commendable, considering the continuous improvement of democratic systems world over.

Master Guan Zhong himself and *Guan Zi* or *Master Guan Zhong's Works*, are historic treasure of human society. They are rising high towards the whole world, from its original place Linzi. How dazzling his culture is. There is an ancient poetry in China, which goes like, people admire Confucius greatly as one stops looking up at a peak. Master Guan and his works, immortal monumental work in the history of mankind, show the intelligent and wisdom of the scholars of the past, giving clear direction to all descendants.

The valleys of Yellow River and Huaihe River bred the Dong Yi culture, which further cultivated the Culture of States Lu and State Qi; How sublime the Confucianism is, a big banner of the Culture of Lu; How great, indeed, the Master Guan Zhong is, an insignia of the Culture of Qi. So there would be no need to mention about the Culture of Lu and Confucianism if without Confucius, and no need to talk about the Culture of Qi if without Master Guan Zhong.

目 录

管子生平系年
Master Guan Zhong's Lifetime Chronology

简子生平传略图谱

管子生平传略图谱

王京龙／文
夏晓慧／译

管子生平轨迹图

Master Guan Zhong's Lifetime Pictures Story

01 颍上降生

　　传说管仲生于戊午年戊午月戊午日的午时。据推算，他当是公元前735（丙午）年6（壬午）月6（甲午）日（阴历五月初一日）正晌午时，出生于今安徽省颍上县颍河岸边的管谷村。取名芒种。

A Native of Yingshang

At the noon on June 6th, the May 1st in lunar calendar, it was said Guan Zhong was born at Guangu Village, Yingshang County, in today's Anhui Province. He was named Mangzhong then.

颍上降生

管子生平轨迹图

郭振华／绘

3

管子生平传略图谱

王京龙／文
夏晓慧／译

02 四岁丧父

公元前732年，传说芒种的父亲染病身亡，这年他刚好四岁。

Lost His Father at Four

In 732 BC, it was said that Guan Zhong's father was infected with a disease and then died when Guan Zhong was four years old.

四歲喪父

郭振华／绘

03 八岁入学

　　芒种八岁的时候，就与比他大两岁的好伙伴鲍叔牙一同上学了。按其家族排行，母亲为之取名仲，称为管仲。

Got His Schooling at Eight

When Mangzhong was eight years old, he went to school together with his friend Bao Shuya, who was two years older than him. Then he was renamed Zhong (means the 2nd in Chinese) by his mother, according to the family seniority among brothers and sisters.

八歳入学

管子生平轨迹图

郭振华／绘

04 作诗明志

> 管仲上学三年，十一岁时就写出了《仁义论》一文，并在文章后面题了一首诗："仁义治天下，农桑是根本；国正人心顺，强国先富民。"

High Ambitions with His Poem

It was said that when Guan Zhong was 11 years old, he wrote an article entitled *On Kindheartedness and Justice*, with one poem ended the paper as the following: to manage well your land with kindheartedness and justice, farming and sericulture is fundamental; when national affairs is justified, all people will follow suit; by enriching your people first, your nation will be enriched as well.

作诗明志

长念救治天下苍生
是根本国必以人心
顺强国先富民

05 南阳经商

　　传说管仲十六岁开始，与鲍叔牙开始往来于泰山以南地区经商。管仲曰："吾始困时，尝与鲍叔贾，分财利多自与，鲍叔不以我为贪，知我贫也。吾尝为鲍叔谋事而更穷困，鲍叔不以我为愚，知时有利不利也。吾尝三仕三见逐於君，鲍叔不以我为不肖，知我不遭时也。吾尝三战三走，鲍叔不以我怯，知我有老母也。公子纠败，召忽死之，吾幽囚受辱，鲍叔不以我为无耻，知我不羞小节而耻功名不显于天下也。生我者父母，知我者鲍子也。"史称管鲍之交。

Opening a Business in Nanyang

It is said that at age 16, Guan Zhong started opening a business, with his friend Bao Shuya, and went back and forth to southern area of Mount Taishan. Guan said, "when I was poor and started a business with Bao, I often shared more wealth and profit. Bao knew I was badly in need; I once planned matters for Bao, but made it from bad to worse. He knew that I was not a fool and there was a time of beneficial to wait; I was an officer for three times but expelled by the ruler. Bao didn't thought I was unworthy. He knew that I didn't meet my chance; I fought in three wars and escaped. He knew that I was not timid, as I had my old mother waiting at home. When Prince Jiu failed to take the throne, Zhao Hu died for him. I was a prisoner and was insulted. He knew that what shamed me most is my scholarly honour or official rank not air to the public. He believed that I was not somebody impudence. It is my parents who gave me my life, but it is Bao Shuya who knew me best." Thus in Chinese history we call this a bosom friendship between Guan Zhong and Bao Shuya, something like the friendship of Damon and Pythias.

南陽經商

郭振华／绘

11

管子生平传略图谱

王京龙／文
夏晓慧／译

06 入士齐国

传说管仲二十五岁的时候，与鲍叔牙一同离开颍上来到了齐国。这时候的齐国就有"小伯春秋"的美誉了。

Taking an Official Post at State Qi

It is said that at age 25, Guan Zhong came to State Qi with his bosom friend Bao Shuya, from his native Yingshang County. At this time, State Qi enjoys a good reputation of primitive prosperous time.

八士齐国

管子生平轨迹图

郭振华／绘

07　齐国鼎足

　　管仲、鲍叔、召忽是齐国当时的三位大贤。召忽曰："吾三人之于齐国也，譬之犹鼎之有足也，去一则不立矣。"

Three Key Figures Making State Qi the Greatest

Guan Zhong, Bao Shuya and Zhao Hu were three key figures in State Qi. Zhao Hu once said, "What we three people to our state is just like foots to a tripot. If one foot is eliminated, the pot will collapse."

08 傅公子纠

　　齐僖公二十九年，齐僖公为他的两个儿子选定了"傅"，相当于现在的导师。管仲、召忽傅公子纠，鲍叔牙傅小白。这年管仲三十岁，鲍叔牙三十二岁。

A Tutor to Prince Jiu

At the 29th year of Duke Xi of Qi, Duke Xi selected retainers respectively for his two sons. The retainer is somebody like a tutor and advisor today. Guan Zhong and Zhao Hu were for Prince Jiu, while Bao Shuya was for Prince Xiaobai. Guan was 30 years old that year and Bao was 32.

傅公子纠

09 辅纠奔鲁

齐襄公是个无道昏君，他的两个弟弟害怕祸及自身，都出走了。公子纠在管仲和召忽的辅佐下投奔去了鲁国，公子小白在鲍叔牙的辅佐下投奔去了莒国。

Assisting Prince Jiu to Go to State Lu

Duke Xiang of Qi was a fatuous and self-indulgent ruler. His two younger brothers were afraid of being hurt by him, both ran away. Prince Jiu went to State Lu for shelter, together with his retainers Guan Zhong and Zhao Hu; Prince Xiaobai went to State Ju for shelter with his retainer Bao Shuya.

辅纠奔鲁

管子生平轨迹图

郭振华／绘

管子生平传略图谱

王京龙／文
夏晓慧／译

⑩ 一箭之仇

　　齐襄公死后，公子纠与公子小白争夺齐国君位。管仲射公子小白中钩，结下一箭之仇。

Hatred Because of an Arrow

After the death of Duke Xiang of Qi, Princes Jiu and Xiaobai fought for the throne of Qi. On his way back to State Qi, Guan Zhong intended to kill Prince Xiaobai with an arrow but hit at his belt hook. Thus Prince Xiaobai hated Guan Zhong.

一箭之仇

管子生平轨迹图

郭振华／绘

⑪ 鲍叔力荐

　　齐桓公做国君后，要拜鲍叔牙为国相，鲍叔牙则力荐管仲为齐国国相。鲍叔牙辞曰："臣，君之庸臣也。君有加惠于其臣，使臣不冻饥，则是君之赐也。若必治国家，则非臣之所能也，其唯管夷吾乎。臣之所不如管夷吾者五：宽惠爱民，臣不如也；治国不失秉，臣不如也；忠信可结于诸侯，臣不如也；制礼义可法于四方，臣不如也；介胄执枹，立于军门，使百姓皆加勇，臣不如也。夫管仲，民之父母也，将欲治其子，不可弃其父母。"

Forceful Recommendation by Bao Shuya

After Prince Xiaobai became the king of State Qi, he intended to nominate Bao as his prime minister. Bao didn't accept this and recommended forcefully his bosom friend Guan Zhong instead. He declined the nomination with the following words: "I am only a second-rate officer. Your lordship gives your kindness to me and makes my life comfortable. But as for managing governance well, I am not good at that. It is only Guan Yiwu who is a talent for this. He has the following five qualities: his broad kindness to our people; ruling the state according to law; being loyal and sincere to unit those dukes or princes; establishing etiquette system for all to follow; putting on a suit of armour and beating a drum to encourage our people. All these five things, he will do much better than me. Guan Zhong is just like a parent to our people. So now, if you want to take care of your sons and daughters well, you can't abandon their parent."

管子生平传略图谱

王京龙／文
夏晓慧／译

鲍叔力荐

管子生平轨迹图

郭振华／绘

12 管仲归齐

齐国大军逼迫战败的鲁国杀死了公子纠，召忽自杀，管仲得以被解救回齐。

Guan Zhong Returned to State Qi

Huge army of Qi coerced the defeated State Lu into killing the Prince Jiu, and his retainer Zhao Hu committed suicide for his master; Guan Zhong was rescued and went back to State Qi.

管仲归齐

13 义答封人

　　管仲作为囚徒来到齐国边境，向边关官员乞求饮食。边境官员封人素知管仲大名，今日虽然为囚，前途不可限量，于是"封人跪而食之，甚敬"。并趁机对管仲说："你现在是囚徒，我这样招待你，将来你有权有势了怎样报答我呢？"管仲回答说："如果我真能如你所愿，并没有特殊的本事报答你，你有贤德我会重用你，你有才能我会给你合适的岗位，你有功劳我会给你应得的奖赏。"

Dutiful Reply to the Officer at Frontier Juncture

As a prisoner, Guan Zhong was on his way back to his state. Being hungry, he begged for something to drink and eat from the officer at the frontier juncture. The officer knew Guan Zhong's name well, thought that today he was a prisoner, but he had a very promising future. So the officer kneed down in a respectful way to offer food to Guan, and asked Guan that, "I served you in such a respectful way today, though you were a prisoner. In what way would you pay back when you were powerful and influential later?" Guan replied, "if I would be what you expected later, I had no special ability to pay back you. If you had good and honest virtue, I would put you in an important position; if you were talent, I would give you a fitting post and would reward you for your outstanding contribution."

義管封人

管子生平轨迹图

郭振华／绘

27

王京龙 / 文
夏晓慧 / 译

14 管仲拜相

管仲五十一岁这年，被齐桓公拜为齐国国相。

Nominated Prime Minister with a Grand Ceremony at a Platform

When Guan Zhong was 51 years old, he was nominated by Duke Huan as the prime minister of State Qi, with a grand ceremony at a specially built high platform.

管仲拜相

15 桓管治国

　　齐桓公拜管仲为相，在设计治国目标时，齐桓公要"安社稷"，管仲坚持要"霸天下"。"君霸王，社稷定。"

Ruling Under Duke Huan and Guan Zhong

After Duke Huan of Qi did obeisance to nominate Guan Zhong as his prime minister with a grand ceremony, he made a point of stabilizing his state as his main objective. While Guan Zhong, instead, was intent on Duke Huan to be the Conqueror under the sun. "If you obtain the dominant position among all feudal princes, your state will be stable and prosperous."

管子生平轨迹图

郭振华／绘

16 区直相宜

"桓公观于厩，问厩吏曰：厩何事最难？厩吏未对，管仲对曰：夷吾尝为圉人矣，傅马栈最难。先傅曲木，曲木又求曲木，曲木已傅，直木无所施矣。先傅直木，直木又求直木，直木已傅，曲木亦无所施矣。"

Crooked or Straight, That is the Question

Duke Huan of Qi observed a stable, and asking the horse breeding officer, "What is the most difficult thing to do at the stable?" Before he replied, Guan Zhong said, "I used to be a stableman. The most difficult thing for me is to build the stockade: if you select crooked batten first, you have to select another crooked batten to match. So all the crooked battens will be used and all straight ones will be left. If you select straight battens first, then all straight battens match well and the crooked ones will be left. Like attracts like."

曲直相宜

管子生平轨迹图

郭振华／绘

33

17 索要"三权"

　　齐桓公四年。管仲为了能够政令通畅，则向齐桓公要贵、富、亲"三权"。孔子说："管仲之贤，而不得此三权者，亦不能使其君南面而霸矣。"

Demanding "Three Key Rights"

At the 4th year of Duke Huan of Qi, in order to make his government decree unobstructed, Guan Zhong demanded three key rights from Duke Huan, namely leadership, financial and administrative authority. Confucius later commented that Guan Zhong was a talent in managing State Qi affairs. Without these three key rights entrusted, he wouldn't have made his lord facing to the south—to be a lord protector.

18 为政之宝

政之所兴，在顺民心。政之所废，在逆民心。故知"予之为取者，政之宝也"。

A Key to Successful Governance

A key to successful governance is to follow the common aspiration of the people and vice versa. Therefore, knowing that giving is for gaining is important for governing political affairs.

為政之寶

19 国之四维

"国有四维，一维绝则倾，二维绝则危，三维绝则覆，四维绝则灭。倾可正也，危可安也，覆可起也，灭不可复错也。何谓四维？一曰礼，二曰义，三曰廉，四曰耻。"

The Four Cardinal Ethics

A state has four cardinal ethics. If one is eliminated, the state will totter; if two, it will be in danger; if three, it will be overthrown. If all the four are eliminated, it will be totally destroyed. What totters may be set straight, what is endangered may be made safe. What has been overthrown may be re-established. But what has been totally destroyed can never be restored. What are these four cardinal ethics? The first is etiquette, the second is righteousness, the third is integrity and the fourth is a sense of shame.

20 定民之居

桓公"恐宗庙之不扫除，社稷之不血食"。管仲对之以"定民之居，成民之事"，提出"士农工商，国之石民也"。

House Settlement

Duke Huan "really worries that nobody will sweep my ancestral temple often, and nobody offers sacrifice to my tract of land." Guan Zhong replied that, "Only to stabilize the housing of people, and arrange occupations well." He further pointed out that "scholars, farmers, craftsmen and merchants are the mainstay of a state."

定民之居

21 修旧之法

桓公"与从事于天下诸侯"。管仲对之以"修旧法，择其善者，举而严用之"。

Amendment to Laws

Duke Huan of Qi intended to employ himself in serving all feudal princes, Guan Zhong replied that, "you need to amend those past laws, select and apply those right clauses to execute to the letter."

修盖之法

22 缘陵封杞

宋国伐杞国，齐"桓公筑缘陵以封之，予车百乘，甲一千"。

To Enfeoff Small State Qi at Yuanling

State Song invaded small State Qi (杞). So Duke Huan had Yuanling City built as a fief for the small Qi (杞), together with 100 chariots and 1,000 soldiers with armour.

缘陵封杞

23 夷仪封邢

"狄人伐邢，邢君出致于齐，桓公筑夷仪以封之，予车百乘，卒千人。"

To Enfeoff State Xing at Yiyi

Minority Di occupied State Xing. The leader of State Xing fled to state Qi. Duke Huan had Yiyi City built as a fief to Xing, together with 100 chariots and 1000 soldiers.

管子生平轨迹图

郭振华／绘

简
子
生
平
传
略
图
谱

管子生平传略图谱

王京龙／文
夏晓慧／译

24 楚丘封卫

狄人伐卫，卫君出致于虚，"桓公筑楚丘以封之，与车三百乘，甲五千。"

To Enfeoff State Wei at Chuqiu

Minority Di occupied State Wei. The leader of Wei fled to Xu (a city in State Qi). Duke Huan had Chuqiu City built as a fief to Wei, together with 300 chariots and 5000 soldiers with armour.

楚丘封卫

25 首霸诸侯

　　齐桓公与宋桓公、陈宣公、卫惠公、郑厉公、单伯会于鄄（juàn）。齐桓公从此开始称霸诸侯。

The First and Most Prominent Lord Protector

Duke Huan had a summit meeting at Juan, in today's Heze City, with Duke Huan of Song, Duke Xuan of Chen, Duke Hui of Wei, Duke Li of Zheng, also with a minister Shan Bo from Western Zhou Dynasty. From then on, Duke Huan started his lord protector duty.

王京龙／文
夏晓慧／译

管子生平轨迹图

管仲
首霸诸侯
齐桓公
郑厉公
宋桓公
陈宣公
卫惠公
单伯

26 官山与海

桓公问于管子曰："吾欲藉于台雉何如？"管子对曰："此毁成也。""吾欲藉于树木？"管子对曰："此伐生也。""吾欲藉于六畜？"管子对曰："此杀生也。""吾欲藉于人，何如？"管子对曰："此隐情也。"桓公曰："然则吾何以为国？"管子对曰："唯官山海为可耳。"创造了"关市几而不征"的税收优惠政策。

State Monopoly Policy Over Salt and Iron

Duke Huan inquired Guan Zhong, "I want to levy tax on real estate. What is your opinion?" "That will make people tear down their housing." replied Guan. "How about levying tax on wood and trees?" Duke Huan asked again. "People will fell trees, even they are young." "How about levying tax on domestic animals?" "Then all young animals will be killed." "So what about levying tax on each person?" "That will then reduce our population." "So what else can I do to enrich my state?" Duke inquired again. "To levy tax on salt and iron." Then the tax preferential policy was applied. Goods were inspected at checkpoints and markets without taxation.

管山与海

管子生平轨迹图

郭振华／绘

27 老马识途

管仲、隰朋从于桓公而伐孤竹，春往冬反，迷途失道。管仲曰：
"老马之智可用也。"乃放老马而随之，遂得道。

An Old Horse Knows the Way Back Home

Led by Duke Huan of Qi, Guan Zhong and Xi Peng dispatched an
expedition against minority Guzhu in spring. When they went back in winter,
they got lost on way home. Guan Zhong said, "we might try to depend on the
wit of an old horse." so they let go the old horse and followed its trace. Finally
they found the right way.

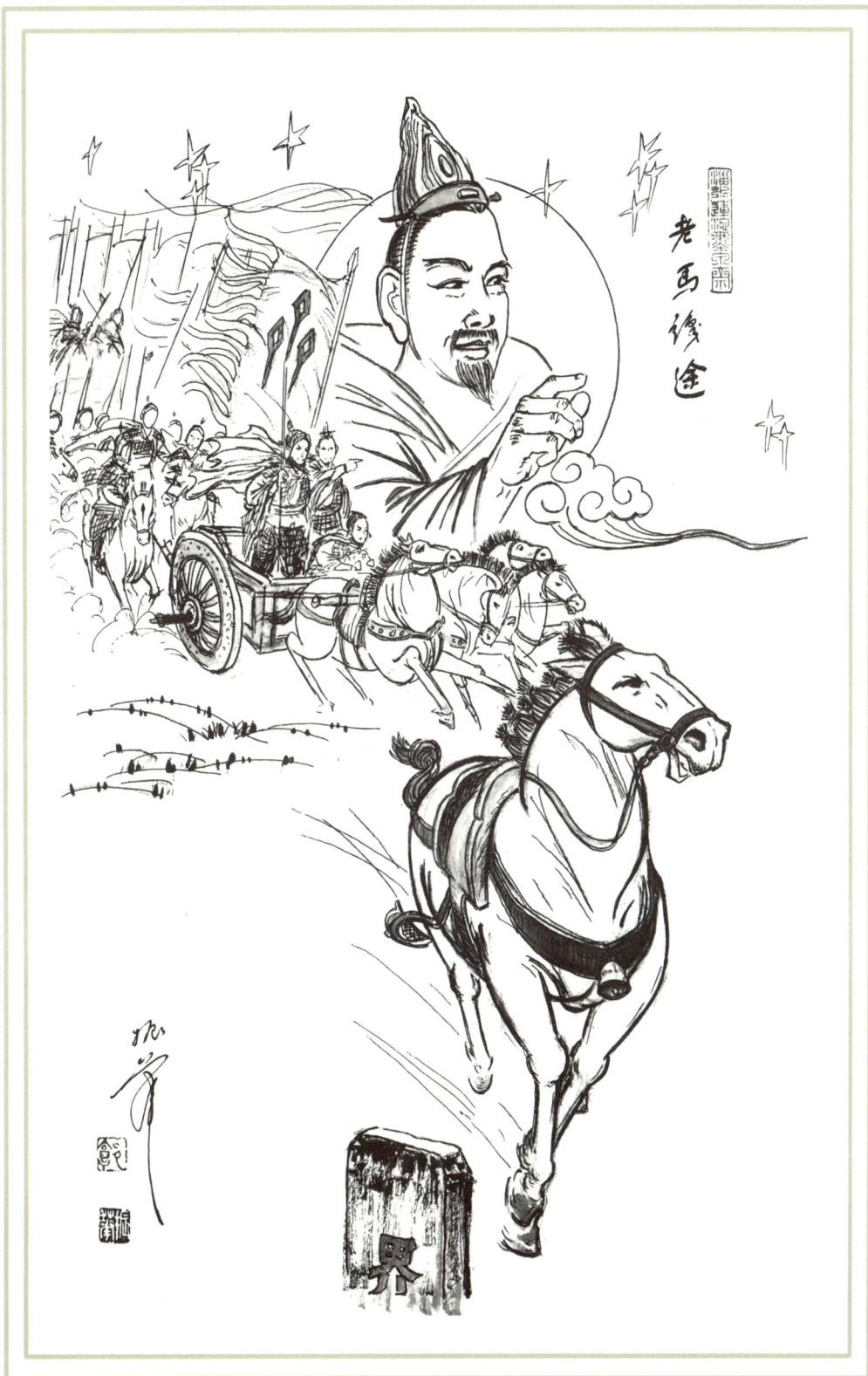

老马修途

管子生平轨迹图

郭振华／绘

28 筑城小谷

齐桓公为管仲筑城小谷，以答谢管仲的功绩。《左传》说："凡邑，有宗庙先君之主曰都，无曰邑。邑曰筑，都曰城。"

City-built at Xiaogu

Duke Huan had a city Xiaogu built to express his appreciation for Guan Zhong's merits and achievements. According to *Zuo's Commentary on Spring and Autumn Annals*, "a settlement with ancestral temples or a lord of a late emperor is called a capital; if not, it is just a town."

筑城山谷

管子生平轨迹图

郭振华／绘

57

29 家有"三归"

> 或曰："管仲俭乎？"曰："管氏有三归，官事不摄，焉得俭？"

Three Real Estates

Someone asked, "Did Guan Zhong display an example of frugality?"
Confucius said, "Guan had three real estates while disregarded official affair.
How can he be cited as an example of frugality?"

金库

家有『三归』

孔子

管子生平轨迹图

郭振华／绘

30 "塞门""反坫"

"然则管仲知礼乎？"曰："邦君树塞门，管氏亦树塞门；邦君为两君之好，有反坫（diàn），管氏亦有反坫。管氏而知礼，孰不知礼？"

To Mask Gate, To Use Cup Stand, a Prince Prerogation

"But did Guan Zhong have a great knowledge of propriety?" Confucius said, "Only a prince of a state may build a screen to mask his gate, but Guan had such a screen. Only the prince of a state, when meeting another such prince, may use a stand for turned-down cups; but Guan also used one. If one could act like Guan Zhong and still be considered to know the propriety, then who else couldn't be?"

管子生平轨迹图

郭振华／绘

31 夺伯氏邑

子曰："（管仲）人也。夺伯氏骈邑三百，饭疏食，没齿，无怨言。"

Confiscation of a Town From Senior Official Bo Family

Confucius said, "Guan Zhong was a person of ability, fairness and justice. Although he confiscated Pianyi, a town of three hundred households, from senior official Bo, the latter was reduced to coarse diet. To his dying day, the latter did not utter one word of resentment against Guan Zhong."

管子生平轨迹图

郭振华／绘

32 义存卫国

狄人灭卫，齐国赠卫文公乘马四匹，祭服五称，牛、羊、豕、鸡、狗皆三百，与门材，赠卫文公夫人鱼轩（小车）重锦三十匹。

Dutiful Saving the State Wei

Troops of minority Di had State Wei perished. Marquis of Qi presented Duke Wen of Wei four saddle horses and vestments of five suits; livestock including cows, sheep, pigs, chickens, and dogs, each of 300; doors-making materials; and presented Duchess an elegant wooden vehicle with roof decorated with skin of fish, and brocade of about 1,000 meters.

义存衛国

管子生平轨迹图

郭振华／绘

33 蔡姬荡舟

　　齐桓公与蔡姬游，蔡姬荡舟，桓公惧而逐蔡姬于蔡，蔡公令其改嫁，桓公怒，欲伐蔡，管仲建议改为伐楚。

Cai Ji Boating

Duke Huan and his wife Cai Ji strolled about, boating at a park. Cai Ji waggled the boat joking on purpose and Duke Huan was frightened but couldn't stop her. In a rage, Duke Huan let Cai Ji go back to State Cai. But Cai Ji's brother, Duke Mu of Cai was not happy and had his sister remarried. Duke Huan was so angry that he wanted to attack the State Cai.

Guanzhong adviced to attack the State Chu instead.

34 召陵之盟

　　齐侯以诸侯之师侵蔡。蔡溃，遂伐楚。楚子使与师言曰："君处北海，寡人处南海，唯是风马牛不相及也，不虞君之涉吾地也，何故？"管仲对曰："昔召康公命我先君大公曰：'五侯九伯，女实征之，以夹辅周室！'赐我先君履，东至于海，西至于河，南至于穆陵，北至于无棣。尔贡包茅不入，王祭不共，无以缩酒，寡人是征。昭王南征而不复，寡人是问。"对曰："贡之不入，寡君之罪也，敢不共给？昭王之不复，君其问诸水滨！"齐楚订立召陵之盟。

Alliance at Zhaoling

United troops of feudal princes under Duke Huan invaded state Cai and got it badly defeated. So the troop further descended upon Chu. An envoy of Chu came and said to the Duke Huan: "Your Lordship is governing the north area, whereas my lord is governing the south area. So this is something entirely not related each other. However your lordship has made a long and difficult journey to my state. What is the reason for you doing so?" Guan Zhong replied, "Once, Lord Kang of Zhou gave orders to our late father, founder of State Qi, Jiang Taigong, that in order to support the House of Zhou, you are authorised to go on a punitive expedition against any guilty of those feudal princes of all the five degrees and the chiefs of all nine provinces, to rule over a tract of land of east to the sea, west to the Yellow River, south to the Muling, and north to the Wudi. Your lord is required to pay tribute bundled thatch for the King of Zhou's prerogative sacrifice.You didn't provide that, so the King of Zhou has no bundled thatch to filter the sacrificial wine. That is why I came here to inquire. Also King Zhao of Zhou hasn't returned from his southern tour and I have to inquire about the reason." The envoy replied, "Articles of tribute hasn't arrive on time, this is the fault of my lord. We dare not delay providing this tribute. As for the reason why King Zhao didn't return, you have to inquire it at banks of river." At last Qi and Chu had an alliance at Zhaoling.

召陵之盟

35 葵丘大会

齐桓公三十五年，齐桓公邀请鲁、宋、卫、郑、许、曹等诸侯葵丘会盟，周襄王派周公宰参加。

General Meeting at Kuiqiu

At the 35th year of Duke Huan of Qi, Duke Huan invited feudal princes from Lu, Song, Wei, Zheng, Xu, Cao, etc. to form an alliance at Kuiqiu. Minister Zai from Zhou attended on behalf of King Xiang of Western Zhou Dynasty.

葵丘大會

36 管仲循礼

齐桓公三十八年，管仲为周、晋调和矛盾，周天子欲以上卿之礼飨管仲，管仲以下卿之礼受之："臣贱有司也，有天子之二守国、高在，若节春秋来承王命，何以礼焉。陪臣敢辞？"

Guan Zhong Abiding by the Rite

At the 38th year of Duke Huan of Qi, Guan Zhong reconciled the contradiction between Western Zhou Dynasty and State Jin. King Zhou, Son of Heaven, intended with thanks to treat Guan Zhong as a higher rank official. Guan Zhong didn't accept such honor, instead he accepted as a normal official rite and said, "Thanks for your kindness. I am just a lower-rank officer. This suits me well. There are two higher rank officials, namely Guo clan and Gao clan, in my state, when they come to pay tribute to your Lordship, at spring time or autumn season, they deserve that entertainment. Sorry I am your humble vassal. I have to decline that."

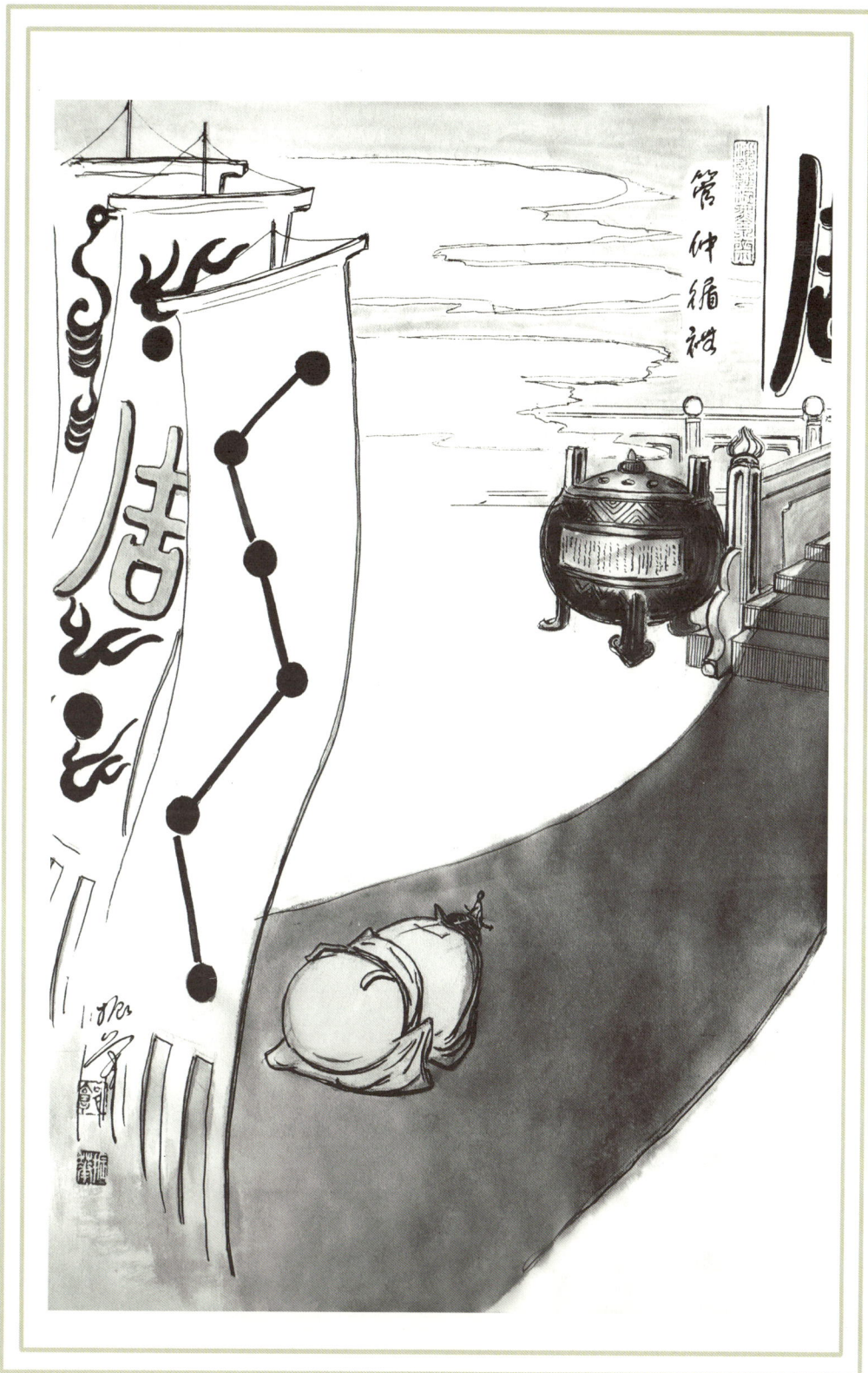

管子生平轨迹图

郭振华／绘

管子生平传略图谱

王京龙/文
夏晓慧/译

37 病榻论相

管仲有病，齐桓公管仲病榻论相，管仲荐隰朋而不荐鲍叔牙。

Last Admonishing on Governance at Sickbed

During his serious illness, Guan Zhong admonished Duke Huan, who came visiting him at sickbed, to have Xi Peng to be his successor, not recommending his bosom friend Bao Shuya for the post.

病榻论相

鲍叔牙

管子生平轨迹图

郭振华／绘

75

38 谏逐佞侍

  管仲建议齐桓公将身边的易牙、竖刁、公子开方、堂巫等佞侍尽行驱逐。

Expelling Flattery Courtiers

For the sake of State Qi after his death, Guan Zhong suggested to have those flattery courtiers like Yi Ya, Shu Diao, Prince Kaifang of Wei, and Tang Zhiwu all expelled.

管子生平轨迹图

郭振华／绘

管子生平轨迹图

郭振华／绘

39 魂归牛山

齐桓公四十一年，管仲死，葬于牛山之下，享年91岁。

Niushan Hill, His Final Resting Place

At the 41th year of Duke Huan of Qi, Master Guan Zhong died at the age of 91, and was buried at the foot of Niushan Hill.

魂归牛山

40 世祀之享

《左传》记载说，君子曰："管氏之世祀也宜哉！ 让不忘其上。"

Enjoying Generations Respectful Sacrifice

In *Zuo's Commentary on Spring and Autumn Annals*, a man of noble character said, "How appropriate it is, to let Master Guan enjoy generations respectful sacrifice. How humble Guan is, always remembering those higher rank officials."

世祀之享

春秋左传

春秋左传

郭振华／绘

81

管子生平系年

Master Guan Zhong's Lifetime Chronology

本系年综合参考了近代以来众多关于管仲系年的版本，在陈书仪先生《管子大传》（齐鲁书社，2008年版）中的"管仲纪年"基础上，结合自己的认识编订而成。尽管对管仲生平系年的这一排列在论据的采用和历史事实的定位中还会有很多的争议，但我们相信，这是目前最为详细且又大致合理的一种排列结果。对于其中对引用众多学贤的观点，因各方面原因的限制，不及——列出，谨致歉意，并表示真诚致谢。

Referring to many versions of the Guan Zhong's lifetime chronology studies in the modern time, based on the "Guan Zhong's Chronology" in Mr. Chen Shuyi's *Biography of Master Guan Zhong* (Qilu Publishing House, 2008 edition), Master Guan Zhong's Lifetime Chronology is compiled by combining with my own understanding. Although there is a lot of controversy about the adoption of arguments and the positioning of historical facts in this arrangement of Guan Zhong's lifetime chronology, we believed that this is the most detailed and reasonable arrangement for the time being. Some various reasons and citations from scholars' views were not listed completely. So I would like to express my sincere gratitude to them if any omission unexpected.

简子生平传略图谱

管子生平传略图谱

王京龙／文
夏晓慧／译

公元前737年（甲辰），齐庄公五十八年
传说鲍叔牙出生。鲍叔牙1岁。

737 BC (Jiachen Period), the 58th Year of Duke Zhuang of Qi
It is said that Bao Shuya was born in this year. He was 1 years old.

公元前736年（乙巳），齐庄公五十九年
鲍叔牙2岁。

736 BC (Yisi Period), the 59th Year of Duke Zhuang of Qi
Bao Shuya was 2 years old.

公元前735年（丙午），齐庄公六十年
鲍叔牙3岁。
6月（壬午）6日（甲午）日正（午时）（阴历五月初一日中午，此日恰为"芒种"节），传说管仲生于今安徽省颍上县管谷村，取名"芒种"。管仲1岁。

735 BC (Bingwu Period), the 60th Year of Duke Zhuang of Qi
Bao Shuya was 3 years old.
At the noon on June 6th, May 1st in lunar calendar (the Day of Grain in that year), it was said that Guan Zhong was born at a Guangu Village, Yingshang County, in today's Anhui Province. He was named Mangzhong then. Mr. Guan Zhong was 1 years old.

公元前734年（丁未），齐庄公六十一年
管仲2岁，鲍叔牙4岁。

管子生平系年

郭振华／绘

734 BC (Dingwei Period), the 61st Year of Duke Zhuang of Qi

Guan was 2 years old. Bao was 4 years old.

公元前733年（戊申），齐庄公六十二年

管仲3岁，鲍叔牙5岁。

733 BC (Wushen Period), the 62nd Year of Duke Zhuang of Qi

Guan was 3 years old. Bao was 5 years old.

公元前732年（己酉），齐庄公六十三年

管仲4岁，鲍叔牙6岁。

传说芒种4岁时父亲染病身亡。

732 BC (Jiyou Period), the 63rd Year of Duke Zhuang of Qi

Guan was 4 years old. Bao was 6 years old.

It was said that Guan Zhong's father was infected with a disease and died when Guan was 4 years old.

公元前731年（庚戌），齐庄公六十四年

管仲5岁，鲍叔牙7岁。

731 BC (Gengxu Period), the 64th Year of Duke Zhuang of Qi

Guan was 5 years old. Bao was 7 years old.

公元前730年（辛亥），齐僖公元年

管仲6岁，鲍叔牙8岁。

730 BC (Xinhai Period), the 1st year of Duke Xi of Qi

Guan was 6 years old. Bao was 8 years old.

公元前729年（壬子），齐僖公二年
管仲7岁，鲍叔牙9岁。

729 BC (Renzi Period), the 2nd year of Duke Xi of Qi
Guan was 7 years old. Bao was 9 years old.

公元前728年（癸丑），齐僖公三年
管仲8岁，鲍叔牙10岁。
传说这年管仲与鲍叔牙开始读书。

728 BC (Guichou Period), the 3rd year of Duke Xi of Qi
Guan was 8 years old. Bao was 10 years old.
It was said that Guan and Bao started their schooling this year.

公元前727年（甲寅），齐僖公四年
管仲9岁，鲍叔牙11岁。

727 BC (Jiayin Period), the 4th year of Duke Xi of Qi
Guan was 9 years old. Bao was 11 years old.

公元前726年（乙卯），齐僖公五年
管仲10岁，鲍叔牙12岁。

726 BC (Yimao Period), the 5th year of Duke Xi of Qi
Guan was 10 years old. Bao was 12 years old.

管子生平系年

郭振华／绘

公元前725年（丙辰），齐僖公六年

管仲11岁，鲍叔牙13岁。

传说管仲上学三年，写出了"仁义论"一文，并在文章后面题诗一首："仁义治天下，农桑是根本；国政人心顺，强国先富民。"

725 BC (Bingchen Period), the 6th year of Duke Xi of Qi

Guan was 11 years old. Bao was 13 years old.

It is said that when Guan wrote an article entitled *On Kindheartedness and Justice*, with one poem ended the paper as the following: to manage well your land with kindheartedness and justice, farming and sericulture is fundamental; when national affairs is justified, all people will follow suit; by enriching your people first, your nation will be enriched as well.

公元前724年（丁巳），齐僖公七年

管仲12岁，鲍叔牙14岁。

724 BC (Dingsi Period), the 7th year of Duke Xi of Qi

Guan was 12 years old. Bao was 14 years old.

公元前723年（戊午），齐僖公八年

管仲13岁，鲍叔牙15岁。

723 BC (Wuwu Period), the 8th year of Duke Xi of Qi

Guan was 13 years old. Bao was 15 years old.

公元前722年（己未），齐僖公九年

管仲14岁，鲍叔牙16岁。

722 BC (Jiwei Period), the 9th year of Duke Xi of Qi

Guan was 14 years old. Bao was 16 years old.

公元前721年（庚申），齐僖公十年

管仲15岁，鲍叔牙17岁。

721 BC (Gengshen Period), the 10th year of Duke Xi of Qi

Guan was 15 years old. Bao was 17 years old.

公元前720年（辛酉），齐僖公十一年

管仲16岁，鲍叔牙18岁。

小白出生，1岁。

传说管仲与鲍叔牙开始经商。

720 BC (Xinyou Period), the 11th year of Duke Xi of Qi

Guan was 16 years old. Bao was 18 years old. Prince Xiaobai (the 3rd son of Duke Xi) was born in this year.

It is said Guan and Bao started their business then.

公元前719年（壬戌），齐僖公十二年

管仲17岁，鲍叔牙19岁，小白2岁。

719 BC (Renxu Period), the 12th year of Duke Xi of Qi

Guan was 17 years old. Bao was 19 years old. Xiaobai was 2 years old.

公元前718年（癸亥），齐僖公十三年

管仲18岁，鲍叔牙20岁，小白3岁。

718 BC (Guihai Period), the 13rd year of Duke Xi of Qi

Guan was 18 years old. Bao was 20 years old. Xiaobai was 3 years old.

公元前717年（甲子），齐僖公十四年

管仲19岁，鲍叔牙21岁，小白4岁。

齐鲁艾（在今山东省泰安境内）之盟。齐、鲁、宋、卫、郑五国输粮于周救济。

717 BC (Jiazi Period), the 14th year of Duke Xi of Qi

Guan was 19 years old. Bao was 21 years old. Xiaobai was 4 years old.

States Qi and Lu was in alliance at place Ai (in today's Tai'an, Shandong Province). Five states, namely Qi, Lu, Song, Wei and Zheng, transported grain to relief disaster need of Western Zhou Dynasty.

公元前716年（乙丑），齐僖公十五年

管仲20岁，鲍叔牙22岁，小白5岁。

齐僖公派同母弟，夷仲年聘鲁。

716 BC (Yichou Period), the 15th year of Duke Xi of Qi

Guan was 20 years old. Bao was 22 years old. Xiaobai was 5 years old.

Duke Xi of Qi sent his half brother Yi Zhongnian had an official visit to State Lu.

公元前715年（丙寅），齐僖公十六年

管仲21岁，鲍叔牙23岁，小白6岁。

宋殇公、卫宣公与齐僖公盟于瓦屋（在今河南省温县境内）。

《国语·郑语》：齐庄、僖于是乎小霸。

715 BC (Bingyin Period), the 16th year of Duke Xi of Qi

Guan was 21 years old. Bao was 23 years old. Xiaobai was 6 years old.

Duke Shang of Song, Duke Xuan of Wei and Duke Xi of Qi had an alliance meeting in Wawu (within today's Wenxian County, Henan Province). *Discourses of the States*, *the Zheng*: thus an Initial Powerful Chief formed during the ruling of Duke Zhuang and Duke Xi of Qi.

公元前714年（丁卯），齐僖公十七年

管仲22岁，鲍叔牙24岁，小白7岁。

鲁隐公与齐僖公应周王之命会于防（在今山东省费县境内）。

714 BC (Dingmao Period), the 17th year of Duke Xi of Qi

Guan was 22 years old. Bao was 24 years old. Xiaobai was 7 years old.

Following the order from King of Western Zhou Dynasty, Duke Yin of Lu met Duke Xi of Qi at place Fang, which is in today's Feixian, Shandong.

公元前713年（戊辰），齐僖公十八年

管仲23岁，鲍叔牙25岁，小白8岁。

齐僖公、郑庄公、鲁隐公会于中丘（在今山东省临沂境内），盟于邓（在今山东省兰陵境内）。

713 BC (Wuchen Period), the 18th year of Duke Xi of Qi

Guan was 23 years old. Bao was 25 years old. Xiaobai was 8 years old.

Duke Xi of Qi, Duke Zhuang of Zheng, and Duke Yin of Lu met at Zhongqiu, in today's Linyi City, Shandong, and formed alliance at place Deng, in today's Lanling County, Shandong.

公元前712年（己巳），齐僖公十九年

管仲24岁，鲍叔牙26岁，小白9岁。

郑、齐、鲁联合伐许，齐僖公将许国国土让给鲁，鲁隐公不敢接受；让给郑，郑国归还许。

712 BC (Jisi Period), the 19th year of Duke Xi of Qi

Guan was 24 years old. Bao was 26 years old. Xiaobai was 9 years old.

States Zheng, Qi and Lu sent a joint punitive expedition against State Xu. Duke Xi of Qi intended to give the territory of Xu to State Lu. Duke Yin of Lu dared not to accept; then it was given to State Zheng, but Zheng returned it to its original owner Xu.

公元前711年（庚午），齐僖公二十年

管仲25岁，鲍叔牙27岁，小白10岁。

传说管仲与鲍叔牙离开颍上来到齐国。

711 BC (Gengwu Period), the 20th year of Duke Xi of Qi

Guan was 25 years old. Bao was 27 years old. Xiaobai was 10 years old.

It is said that Guan and Bao came to State Qi from their hometown Yingshang.

公元前710年（辛未），齐僖公二十一年

管仲26岁，鲍叔牙28岁，小白11岁。

齐、鲁、陈、郑会于稷（在今河南省商丘境内）。

710 BC (Xinwei Period), the 21st year of Duke Xi of Qi

Guan was 26 years old. Bao was 28 years old. Xiaobai was 11 years old.

Dukes from States Qi, Lu, Chen and Zheng met at place Ji, in today's Shangqiu, Henan Province.

公元前709年（壬申），齐僖公二十二年

管仲27岁，鲍叔牙29岁，小白12岁。

齐僖公、鲁桓公会于嬴（今山东省莱芜境内）。齐文姜嫁于鲁桓公为夫人。

709 BC (Renshen Period), the 22nd year of Duke Xi of Qi

Guan was 27 years old. Bao was 29 years old. Xiaobai was 12 years old.

Duke Xi of Qi met Duke Huan of Lu at place Ying, in today's Laiwu City. Princess Wenjiang of Qi got married with Duke Huan of Lu.

公元前708年（癸酉），齐僖公二十三年

管仲28岁，鲍叔牙30岁，小白13岁。

708 BC (Guiyou Period), the 23rd year of Duke Xi of Qi

Guan was 28 years old. Bao was 30 years old. Xiaobai was 13 years old.

公元前707年（甲戌），齐僖公二十四年

管仲29岁，鲍叔牙31岁，小白14岁。齐侯、郑伯朝于纪（纪国，在齐国东面），欲袭之。纪人知之，齐、郑只好作罢。

707 BC (Jiaxu Period), the 24th year of Duke Xi of Qi

Guan was 29 years old. Bao was 31 years old. Xiaobai was 14 years old. Marquis of Qi and ruler of Zheng went to State Ji, which located at the east of Qi, attempted to raid Ji. When people of Ji knew this plot, hence the plan had to be given up.

公元前706年（乙亥），齐僖公二十五年

管仲30岁，鲍叔牙32岁，小白15岁。

齐襄公与文姜乱伦，管仲劝说，齐襄公不听。齐僖公委派鲍叔牙辅佐公子小白，管仲、召忽辅佐公子纠。

706 BC (Yihai Period), the 25th year of Duke Xi of Qi

Guan was 30 years old. Bao was 32 years old. Xiaobai was 15 years old.

Duke Xiang of Qi got fornication with his sister, Wenjiang, and didn't accept Guan Zhong's persuading. Duke Xi of Qi appointed Bao Shuya, his retainer, to tutor Prince Xiaobai, and retainers Guan Zhong and Zhao Hu to tutor Prince Jiu.

公元前705年（丙子），齐僖公二十六年

管仲31岁，鲍叔牙33岁，小白16岁。

齐襄公与文姜乱伦，管仲劝说，齐襄公不听。齐僖公委派鲍叔牙辅佐公子小白，管仲、召忽辅佐公子纠。

陈敬仲完出生。

705 BC (Bingzi Period), the 26th year of Duke Xi of Qi

Guan was 31 years old. Bao was 33 years old. Xiaobai was 16 years old.

Duke Xiang of Qi got fornication with Wenjiang, and didn't accept Guan Zhong's persuading. Duke Xi of Qi appointed his retainer Bao Shuya to tutor prince Xiaobai, retainers Guan Zhong and Zhao Hu to tutor prince Jiu.

Prince Wan of State Chen, with courtesy name Jingzhong, was born.

公元前704年（丁丑），齐僖公二十七年

管仲32岁，鲍叔牙34岁，小白17岁。

704 BC (Dingchou Period), the 27th year of Duke Xi of Qi

Guan was 32 years old. Bao was 34 years old. Xiaobai was 17 years old.

公元前703年（戊寅），齐僖公二十八年

管仲33岁，鲍叔牙35岁，小白18岁。

703 BC (Wuyin Period), the 28th year of Duke Xi of Qi

Guan was 33 years old. Bao was 35 years old. Xiaobai was 18 years old.

公元前702年（己卯），齐僖公二十九年

管仲34岁，鲍叔牙36岁，小白19岁。

齐侯、卫侯、郑伯与鲁战于郎（在今山东省鱼台）。

702 BC (Jimao Period), the 29th year of Duke Xi of Qi

Guan was 34 years old. Bao was 36 years old. Xiaobai was 19 years old.

Leader of Qi, Leader of Wei, and Earl of Zheng went to war with State Lu at place Lang, in today's Yutai, Shandong.

公元前701年（庚辰），齐僖公三十年

管仲35岁，鲍叔牙37岁，小白20岁。

齐、卫、郑、宋盟于恶曹（或在今河南省延津县境内）。

701 BC (Gengchen Period), the 30th year of Duke Xi of Qi

Guan was 35 years old. Bao was 37 years old. Xiaobai was 20 years old.

Four States, Qi, Wei, Zheng and Song allied at E'Cao, a place might in today's Yanjin County, Henan Province.

公元前700年（辛巳），齐僖公三十一年

管仲36岁，鲍叔牙38岁，小白21岁。

700 BC (Xinsi Period), the 31st year of Duke Xi of Qi

Guan was 36 years old. Bao was 38 years old. Xiaobai was 21 years old.

公元前699年（壬午），齐僖公三十二年

管仲37岁，鲍叔牙39岁，小白22岁。

齐国夷仲年死，齐僖公令其子公孙无知秩服奉养比太子。

齐僖公约会宋、卫、燕四国联合伐纪。

699 BC (Renwu Period), the 32nd year of Duke Xi of Qi

Guan was 37 years old. Bao was 39 years old. Xiaobai was 22 years old.

When his brother, Yi Zhongnian died, Duke Xi of Qi favored Zhongnian's son, his nephew, Gongsun Wuzhi, as a prince, raising his status both in official treatment and uniform class.

Duke Xi of Qi called on three states, Song, Wei and Yan to send a joint punitive expedition against State Ji.

公元前698年（癸未），齐僖公三十三年

管仲38岁，鲍叔牙40岁，小白23岁。

齐僖公死，太子诸儿即位，是为齐襄公。鲍叔牙辅佐公子小白逃往莒国。

698 BC (Guiwei Period), the 33rd year of Duke Xi of Qi

Guan was 38 years old. Bao was 40 year old. Xiaobai was 23 years old.

When Duke Xi of Qi died, his first prince Zhu'er was on the enthronement, that was Duke Xiang of Qi. Bao Shuya assisted Prince Xiaobai escaping to State Ju.

公元前697年（甲申），齐襄公元年

管仲39岁，鲍叔牙41岁，小白24岁。

齐襄公绌公孙无知太子秩服奉养。齐襄公与鲁桓公会于艾。

697 BC (Jiashen Period), the 1st year under Duke Xiang of Qi

Guan was 39 years old. Bao was 41 years old. Xiaobai was 24 years old.

Duke Xiang of Qi dismissed his brother, Prince Gongsun Wuzhi both in his official treatment and uniform class. Duke Xiang of Qi met Duke Huan of Lu at place Ai.

公元前696年（乙酉），齐襄公二年

管仲40岁，鲍叔牙42岁，小白25岁。

卫桓公奔齐。

696 BC (Yiyou Period), the 2nd year of Duke Xiang of Qi

Guan was 40 years old. Bao was 42 years old. Xiaobai was 25 years old.

Duke Huan of State Wei rushed to State Qi for shelter.

公元前695年（丙戌），齐襄公三年

管仲41岁，鲍叔牙43岁，小白26岁。

齐襄公、鲁桓公、纪侯盟于黄（在今山东省淄川境内）。

695 BC (Bingxu Period), the 3rd year of Duke Xiang of Qi

Guan was 41 years old. Bao was 43 years old. Xiaobai was 26 years old.

Duke Xiang of Qi, Duke Huan of Lu and Leader of Ji met for alliance at place Huang, which is in Zichuan, Shandong Province.

公元前694年（丁亥），齐襄公四年

管仲42岁，鲍叔牙44岁，小白27岁。

鲁桓公与夫人文姜如齐，与齐襄公私通，鲁桓公知之，齐襄公拉杀鲁桓公。鲁人责齐，齐襄公杀彭生以谢鲁。

文姜子姬同即位，是为鲁庄公，文姜留齐。

694 BC (Dinghai Period), the 4th year of Duke Xiang of Qi

Guan was 42 years old. Bao was 44 years old. Xiaobai was 27 years old.

When Duke Huan of Lu and his wife Duchess Wenjiang went back to State Qi, Wenjiang had fornication again with her half brother, Duke Xiang; when Duke Huan of Lu got this, Duke Xiang killed Duke Huan of Lu with string. People in Lu blamed State Qi, so Duke Xiang killed his brother, prince Peng Sheng to answer that as apology.

Jitong, Duchess Wenjiang's son, got on the enthronement, that was Duke Zhuang of Lu; Duchess Wenjiang thus kept staying in her home Qi.

公元前693年（戊子），齐襄公五年

管仲43岁，鲍叔牙45岁，小白28岁。

齐师伐纪。

693 BC (Wuzi Period), the 5th year of Duke Xiang of Qi

Guan was 43 years old. Bao was 45 years old. Xiaobai was 28 years old.

Troops from Qi was dispatched an expedition against State Ji.

公元前692年（己丑），齐襄公六年

管仲44岁，鲍叔牙46岁，小白29岁。

文姜会齐侯于禚（在今山东省长清境内）。

简子生平传略图谱

管子生平传略图谱

王京龙／文
夏晓慧／译

692 BC (Jichou Period), the 6th year of Duke Xiang of Qi

Guan was 44 years old. Bao was 46 years old. Xiaobai was 29 years old.

A secret meeting of Duchess Wenjiang and Duke Xiang at place Zhuo, in today's Changqing County, Shandong.

公元前691年（庚寅），齐襄公七年

管仲45岁，鲍叔牙47岁，小白30岁。

齐、鲁两国伐卫。纪季以鄑（在今山东省青州境内）降齐。

691 BC (Gengyin Period), the 7th year of Duke Xiang of Qi

Guan was 45 years old. Bao was 47 years old. Xiaobai was 30 years old.

States Qi and Lu sent a joint punitive expedition against State Wei; a young brother of Marquis of State Ji surrendered to Qi, with his annexed land Xi as a dependency, in today's Qingzhou, Shandong.

公元前690年（辛卯），齐襄公八年

管仲46岁，鲍叔牙48岁，小白31岁。

文姜飨齐侯于祝丘（在今山东省临沂境内）。

齐襄公伐纪，纪君出奔。齐襄公葬纪伯。齐襄公与齐人狩于禚。

690 BC (Xinmao Period), the 8th year of Duke Xiang of Qi

Guan was 46 years old. Bao was 48 years old. Xiaobai was 31 years old.

Wenjiang provided dinner for Marquis of Qi at place Zhuqiu, which is in today's Linyi City, Shandong.

Duke Xiang of Qi sent a punitive expedition against State Ji. The ruler of Ji ran away. Duke Xiang buried the ruler of Ji. Duke Xiang and his army went on a punitive expedition at place Zhuo.

公元前689年（壬辰），齐襄公九年

管仲47岁，鲍叔牙49岁，小白32岁。

文姜至齐私会齐襄公。齐襄公纠合鲁、宋、陈、蔡等国纳卫惠公。

689 BC (Renchen Period), the 9th year of Duke Xiang of Qi

Guan was 47 years old. Bao was 49 years old. Xiaobai was 32 years old.

Wenjiang met Duke Xiang of Qi privately at Qi. Duke Xiang called on four States, Lu, Song, Chen and Cai, to escort Duke Hui of Wei back home.

公元前688年（癸巳），齐襄公十年

管仲48岁，鲍叔牙50岁，小白33岁。

受文姜之请，齐人至鲁归卫宝（战利品）。

688 BC (Guisi Period), the 10th year of Duke Xiang of Qi

Guan was 48 years old. Bao was 50 years old. Xiaobai was 33 years old.

At Wenjiang's request, people of Qi went to Lu, giving back the spoils of war to Wei.

公元前687年（甲午），齐襄公十一年

管仲49岁，鲍叔牙51岁，小白34岁。

文姜会齐侯于防、谷（在今山东省东阿，一说今桓台县唐山）。

687 BC (Jiawu Period), the 11th year of Duke Xiang of Qi

Guan was 49 years old. Bao was 51 years old. Xiaobai was 34 years old.

Wenjiang and Duke Xiang secretly met at Fang and Gu respectively (in Dong'e County, another story said at Tangshan, Huantai County. Both places are in Shandong Province).

公元前686年（乙未），齐襄公十二年

管仲50岁，鲍叔牙52岁，小白35岁。

管仲、召忽辅佐公子纠逃亡到了鲁国。

686 BC (Yiwei Period), the 12th year of Duke Xiang of Qi

Guan was 50 years old. Bao was 52 years old. Xiaobai was 35 years old.

Retainers Guan Zhong and Zhao Hu assisted Prince Jiu fled to State Lu.

公元前685年（丙申），齐桓公元年

管仲51岁，鲍叔牙53岁，齐桓公36岁。

公孙无知等弑杀齐襄公。齐人袭杀公孙无知。鲁桓公伐齐，欲纳公子纠；公子小白入齐，即位齐桓公。齐鲁战于乾时（在今山东省临淄境内），鲁国大败。鲁国杀死齐公子纠，召忽自杀殉难。鲍叔力荐管仲。管仲被囚返齐，任齐国国相。

685 BC (Bingshen Period), the 1st year under Duke Huan of Qi

Guan was 51 years old. Bao was 53 years old. Duke Huan of Qi (Xiaobai) was 36 years old.

Prince Gongsun Wuzhi and his followers murdered Duke Xiang of Qi and made himself the state ruler. Shortly, people in the Qi made a surprise attack on him and killed him. Duke Huan of Lu dispatched an expedition against Qi, intended to help Prince Jiu back his home as the ruler. Prince Xiaobai returned home earlier, so he was on the enthronement, that was Duke Huan of Qi. A war broke out at Qianshi (in today's Linzi, Shandong) between States Qi and Lu, with Lu defeated utterly. So Prince Jiu was killed by Lu, and his retainer Zhao Hu thus committed suicide for his master. Bao Shuya recommended Guan Zhong to Duke Huan of Qi. So Guan Zhong, in prisoner's wooden van, returned from Lu and later was nominated as prime minister of State Qi for four decades.

管子生平系年　郭振华／绘

公元前684年（丁酉），齐桓公二年

管仲52岁，鲍叔牙54岁，齐桓公37岁。

鲁败齐师于长勺（在今山东省莱芜境内）。齐、鲁、宋会盟于郎（在今山东省济宁境内）。

齐国灭谭（在今山东省济南境内）。

684 BC (Dingyou Period), the 2nd year of Duke Huan of Qi

Guan was 52 years old. Bao was 54 years old. Duke Huan was 37 years old.

Troops of Qi was defeated by troops from Lu at Changshao, in today's Laiwu City, Shandong. States Qi, Lu and Song met to form an alliance at place Lang, in today's Jining City, Shandong.

State Qi wiped out small State Tan, in today's Jinan City, Shandong.

公元前683年（戊戌），齐桓公三年

管仲53岁，鲍叔牙55岁，齐桓公38岁。

齐桓公"三岁治定"。齐桓公迎娶周共王之女共姬。

683 BC (Wuxu Period), the 3rd year of Duke Huan of Qi

Guan was 53 years old. Bao was 55 years old. Duke Huan was 38 years old.

Duke Huan of Qi stabilized Qi in three years. He married Gongji, daughter of King Gong of Western Zhou Dynasty.

公元前682年（己亥），齐桓公四年

管仲54岁，鲍叔牙56岁，齐桓公39岁。

齐桓公不听管仲劝告，出兵受挫，幡然醒悟。

管仲向齐桓公要贵、富、亲三权，后来孔子评论说："管仲之贤而不得此三权者，亦不能使其君南面而霸矣。"

682 BC (Jihai Period), the 4th year of Duke Huan of Qi

Guan was 54 yeass old. Bao was 56 years old. Duke Huan was 39 years old.

Duke Huan of Qi didn't follow Guan Zhong's advice and dispatched his troops to wars and suffered setbacks. Then he quickly and completely realized the importance of Guan Zhong.

Guan Zhong demanded three key rights from Duke Huan for his better governance, thus making Duke Huan got dominating position among those Dukes under heaven. The three key rights namely were leadership, financial and administrative authority. Confucius later commented that Guan Zhong was a talent in managing State Qi affairs. Without these three key rights entrusted, he wouldn't have made his lord sitting and facing to the south—to be a lord protector.

公元前681年（庚子），齐桓公五年

管仲55岁，鲍叔牙57岁，齐桓公40岁。

齐国主持"北杏（在今山东省东阿境内）之会"。

伐鲁，鲁与齐会于柯（在今山东省阳谷境内）而有"柯之盟"。

齐桓公筑缘陵以封杞（在今山东省昌乐境内），给予车一百乘，甲士一千。

681 BC (Gengzi Period), the 5th year of Duke Huan of Qi

Guan was 55 years old. Bao was 57 years old. Duke Huan was 40 years old.

State Qi hosted "Beixing Alliance," in today's Dong'e County, Shandong.

State Qi dispatched an expedition against Lu. The two troops later met at place Ke, thus having this Ke Alliance, in today's Yanggu County, Shandong.

Duke Huan of Qi constructed Yuanling City on its land as a fief for tributary Qi (杞), together with 100 war chariots, and 1,000 soldiers with armour. This place is in today's Changle County, Shandong.

公元前680年（辛丑），齐桓公六年

管仲56岁，鲍叔牙58岁，齐桓公41岁。

宋国背叛"北杏之盟"，齐国一方面联合陈国和曹国进行讨伐，另一方面派出使者报告了周天子，请求出兵讨伐。宋国不战而屈服求和。郑厉公复位后立即表示与齐国联盟。齐桓公与宋、卫、郑在鄄（今山东省鄄城一带）会盟，周天子派单伯参加。

680 BC (Xinchou Period), the 6th year of Duke Huan of Qi

Guan was 56 years old. Bao was 58 years old. Duke Huan was 41 years old.

When State Song betrayed the Beixing Alliance, Qi united troops from States Chen and Cao by sending a punitive expedition against Song; and sent envoy reporting to the King of Western Zhou Dynasty, Son of Heaven, asking for permission to suppress the Song. Without fighting, Song surrendered for peace. After Duke Li of Zheng's restoration, he promised at once, to form alliance with Qi. Duke Huan of Qi hold meetings at place Juan, in today's Juancheng, Shandong Province, to form alliance, with States Song, Wei and Zheng. Shan Bo, a representative from King of Western Zhou Dynasty, Son of Heaven, was also participating the meeting.

公元前679年（壬寅），齐桓公七年

管仲57岁，鲍叔牙59岁，齐桓公42岁。

齐与宋、陈、卫、郑等诸侯和单伯在鄄再次会盟。齐桓公于是而霸也。

679 BC (Renyin Period), the 7th year of Duke Huan of Qi

Guan was 57 years old. Bao was 59 years old. Duke Huan was 42 years old.

A second alliance meeting was held at Juan, among Dukes of Qi, Song, Chen, Wei and with a representative minister Shan Bo from King of Western

Zhou Dynasty. Duke Huan of Qi was the head of the ally, thus became the first powerful lord protector over the feudal lords, of the Spring and Autumn Period.

公元前678年（癸卯），齐桓公八年

管仲58岁，鲍叔牙60岁，齐桓公43岁。

齐会宋卫伐郑。

随后，齐、鲁、宋、卫、陈、郑、许盟于幽（在今河南省境内）。

楚国兴师侵郑，以与齐国争夺郑国，开始问鼎中原。

678 BC (Guimao Period), the 8th year of Duke Huan of Qi

Guan was 58 years old. Bao was 60 years old. Duke Huan was 43 years old.

States Qi, together with Song and Wei, sent a punitive expedition against State Zheng.

Later, States Qi, Lu, Song, Wei, Chen, Zheng and Xu formed an alliance at place You, in today's Henan Province.

Southern State Chu sent an army to invade State Zheng, in order to compete with State Qi. Thus Chu started fighting for the tripod in the central plain—attempt to seize the throne.

公元前677年（甲辰），齐桓公九年

管仲59岁，鲍叔牙61岁，齐桓公44岁。

郑国使臣来齐意欲破坏盟约，齐国扣留郑国来使。

677 BC (Jiachen Period), the 9th year of Duke Huan of Qi

Guan was 59 years old. Bao was 61 years old. Duke Huan was 44 years old.

An envoy from Zheng came to State Qi on purpose of breaking the alliance, so the envoy was withhold by Qi.

公元前676年（乙巳），齐桓公十年

管仲60岁，鲍叔牙62岁，齐桓公45岁。

戎侵鲁，鲁庄公追戎于济西。

676 BC (Yisi Period), the 10th year of Duke Huan of Qi

Guan was 60 years old. Bao was 62 years old. Duke Huan was 45 years old.

Minority Rong invaded State Lu. Duke Zhuang of Lu chased Rong far to the west of the Yellow River.

公元前675年（丙午），齐桓公十一年

管仲61岁，鲍叔牙63岁，齐桓公46岁。

文姜自鲁至莒。齐、宋、陈伐鲁。

675 BC (Bingwu Period), the 11th year of Duke Huan of Qi

Guan was 61 years old. Bao was 63 years old. Duke Huan was 46 years old.

Duchess Wenjiang left from Lu to State Ju. States Qi, Song and Chen sent a punitive expedition against Lu.

公元前674年（丁未），齐桓公十二年

管仲62岁，鲍叔牙64岁，齐桓公47岁。

夏，齐大火，宗庙厩库尽毁。冬，齐人伐戎。

674 BC (Dingwei Period), the 12th year of Duke Huan of Qi

Guan was 62 years old. Bao was 64 years old. Duke Huan was 47 years old.

In summer, a big fire ruined the ancestral temple and all stable warehouses of Qi. In winter, troops from Qi was dispatched against northern minority Rong.

管子生平传略图谱

王京龙／文

夏晓慧／译

公元前673年（戊申），齐桓公十三年
管仲63岁，鲍叔牙65岁，齐桓公48岁。
齐文姜死。

673 BC (Wushen Period), the 13th year of Duke Huan of Qi
Guan was 63 years old. Bao was 65 years old. Duke Huan was 48 years old.
Duchess Wenjiang of Qi died.

公元前672年（己酉），齐桓公十四年
管仲64岁，鲍叔牙66岁，齐桓公49岁。
陈国公子完，号敬仲，来奔齐。
齐高奚与鲁盟于防。
鲁庄公到齐议婚。

672 BC (Jiyou Period), the 14th year of Duke Huan of Qi

Guan was 64 years old. Bao was 66 years old. Duke Huan was 49 years old.

Prince Wan of State Chen, with his courtesy name Jingzhong, fled to Qi for shelter.

Marquis Gao of State Qi formed alliance with State Lu at place Fang.

Duke Zhuang of Lu went to Qi to exchange views on his marriage.

公元前671年（庚戌），齐桓公十五年
管仲65岁，鲍叔牙67岁，齐桓公50岁。
鲁庄公到齐观社。
齐与鲁盟于扈（疑在近山东省菏泽境内）。

671 BC (Gengxu Period), the 15th year of Duke Huan of Qi

Guan was 65 years old. Bao was 67 years old. Duke Huan was 50 years old.

Duke Zhuang of Lu went to Qi and watched sacrificial rite offered to land.

Qi and Lu met to form alliance at place Hu (maybe in Heze City, Shandong).

公元前670年（辛亥），齐桓公十六年

管仲66岁，鲍叔牙68岁，齐桓公51岁。

冬，郭（疑在今山东省聊城境内）亡，齐桓公在郭地问郭亡的原因，郭地的父老回答说，郭君善善不能用，恶恶不能去，所以亡。

670 BC (Xinhai Period), the 16th year of Duke Huan of Qi

Guan was 66 years old. Bao was 68 years old. Xiaobai was 51 years old.

In Winter, State Guo, maybe in today's Liaocheng City, Shandong, collapsed. Duke Huan of Qi inquired reasons to the local at Guo. He got the answer from the elder as the following: the ruler of Guo praised those able men but didn't employ them; he hated those evil men but couldn't get rid of them.

公元前669年（壬子），齐桓公十七年

管仲67岁，鲍叔牙69岁，齐桓公52岁。

669 BC (Renzi Period), the 17th year of Duke Huan of Qi

Guan was 67 years old. Bao was 69 years old. Duke Huan was 52 years old.

公元前668年（癸丑），齐桓公十八年

管仲68岁，鲍叔牙70岁，齐桓公53岁。

齐、宋、鲁三国之师伐徐（在今安徽省泗县境内）。

668 BC (Guichou Period), the 18th year of Duke Huan of Qi

Guan was 68 years old. Bao was 70 years old. Duke Huan was 53 years old.

States Qi, Song and Lu send a joint punitive expedition against State Xu, in today's Sixian County, Anhui Province.

管子生平传略图谱

王京龙／文
夏晓慧／译

公元前667年（甲寅），齐桓公十九年
管仲69岁，鲍叔牙71岁，齐桓公53岁。
齐会鲁、宋、陈、郑盟于幽，周惠王赐齐桓公为侯伯，命齐讨伐卫国。
弛关市之征。

667 BC (Jiayin Period), the 19th year of Duke Huan of Qi

Guan was 69 years old. Bao was 71 years old. Duke Huan was 53 years old.

State Qi held a meeting with States Lu, Song, Chen and Zheng to form an alliance at place You. The King Hui of Western Zhou Dynasty granted Duke Huan of Qi as head Marquis of those feudal princes and ordered Qi to sent armed forces to suppress State Wei.

All taxes were reduced to 2% only.

公元前666年（乙卯），齐桓公二十年
管仲70岁，鲍叔牙72岁，齐桓公54岁。
齐桓公讨卫。楚伐郑，齐、鲁、宋救郑。

666 BC (Yimao Period), the 20th year of Duke Huan of Qi

Guan was 70 years old. Bao was 72 years old. Duke Huan was 54 years old.

Duke Huan of Qi sent troops to suppress Wei. Chu sent troops to suppress Zheng. The latter got support and help from Qi, Lu and Song.

公元前665年（丙辰），齐桓公二十一年
管仲71岁，鲍叔牙73岁，齐桓公55岁。

665 BC (Bingchen Period), the 21st year of Duke Huan of Qi

Guan was 71 years old. Bao was 73 years old. Duke Huan was 55 years old.

管子生平系年

郭振华／绘

公元前664年（丁巳），齐桓公二十二年

管仲72岁，鲍叔牙74岁，齐桓公56岁。

齐桓公将伐山戎、孤竹（山戎、孤竹均为古代北方游牧部族，在今河北省北部一带），请助于鲁，鲁许之而不行。

664 BC (Dingsi Period), the 22nd year of Duke Huan of Qi

Guan was 72 years old. Bao was 74 years old. Duke Huan was 56 years old.

Duke Huan of Qi would dispatch an expedition against northern nomad tribes Shanrong and Guzhu (in today's northern area of Hebei Province) and requested assistant from Lu. The ruler of Lu promised but without action.

公元前663年（戊午），齐桓公二十三年

管仲73岁，鲍叔牙75岁，齐桓公57岁。

山戎伐燕，齐桓公救燕，至于孤竹而返。燕庄公送齐桓公入齐境，桓公曰：非天子，诸侯相送不出境，吾不可以无礼于燕。于是分沟割燕君所至之地与燕。于是燕君复修召公之政，纳贡于周，如成康之时。诸侯闻之，皆从之。山戎善种冬葱、戎菽，齐桓公皆移植齐国。鲁未参加。

齐已伐山戎、孤竹，而欲移兵于鲁。管仲曰：不可。诸侯未亲，今又伐远而还诛近邻，邻国不亲，非霸王之道。君之所得山戎之宝器者，中国之所鲜也，不可以不进周公之庙。

663 BC (Wuwu Period), the 23rd year of Duke Huan of Qi

Guan was 73 years old. Bao was 75 years old. Duke Huan was 57 years old.

Shanrong invaded State Yan. Duke Huan of Qi sent troops to help Yan, so far as to Guzhu then returned. Duke Zhuang of Yan saw off Duke Huan far into the territory of Qi. Duke Huan said, according to the rites, I'm not a Son of Heaven, the formality of seeing off between the feudal princes should not exit the frontier. I could not allow this discourtesy of seeing off too far crossing the frontier to Yan. Therefore, he marked the land as the new border with a ditching, where Duke Zhuang of Yan reached and gave all northern part to Yan. After that, ruler of Yan restored the policies of Duke Zhao of West Zhou Dynasty (Duke Zhao was an imperial clan) and started paying tributes to Western Zhou Dynasty, as what was done during Kings Cheng and Kang of Western Zhou Dynasty (1042BC to 1020BC). All feudal princes followed suit when they heard this. People of Shanrong were good at cultivating scallion and beans. Duke Huan had them transplanted into his Kingdom. State Lu didn't participate in this battle.

After troops of Qi suppressed minority Shanrong and Guzhu, and wanted to move troops into State Lu. Guan Zhong stopped that. He said, we were not close with other dukes; now we were far away from and intended to punish the neighbour state, they would keep away from us. This was not the right way for a powerful chief. And all war trophies your lordship acquired were rare in central plain, so it would be wise to offer them to the temple of Duke Zhou of Lu.

公元前662年（己未），齐桓公二十四年

管仲74岁，鲍叔牙76岁，齐桓公58岁。

齐献戎捷于鲁周公之庙。

齐国欲兴师伐莒，齐桓公没有邀请鲁庄公，鲁庄公就下令出兵助战。以补未同齐一起伐山戎之过。

齐筑小谷（在今山东省东阿，一说今桓台县唐山），作为管仲采邑。

齐侯与宋公会于梁丘（在今山东省菏泽境内）。为楚伐郑之故请会于齐。

狄伐邢（在今河北省邢台境内）。

鲁公子庆父如齐。

662 BC (Jiwei Period), the 24th year of Duke Huan of Qi

Guan was 74 years old. Bao was 76 years old. Duke Huan was 58 years old.

State Qi offered war trophies against minority Shanrong to the temple of Duke Zhou of Lu.

State Qi intended to descend upon Ju and Duke Huan didn't invite Duke Zhuang of Lu. Duke Zhuang sent his troops voluntarily to make up for his missing of not suppressing the Shanrong.

Xiaogu City was built by Qi as an fief for Guan Zhong. Xiaogu is in today's Dong'e County. Another story said it is in Tangshan, Huantai County.

Duke Huan met Duke of Song at place Liangqiu, in today's Heze City, Shandong, because State Chu descended upon State Zheng.

Minority Di descended upon State Xing, in today's Xingtai, Hebei Province.

Prince Qingfu of Lu came to State Qi.

公元前661年（庚申），齐桓公二十五年

管仲75岁，鲍叔牙77岁，齐桓公59岁。

齐桓公率宋、曹军救邢，败狄师。

秋，鲁闵公与齐桓公盟于落姑（疑在今山东省平阴县或博兴县）。

冬，齐仲孙湫到鲁国省难，回复齐桓公曰："不去庆父，鲁难未已。"

661 BC (Gengshen Period), the 25th year of Duke Huan of Qi

Guan was 75 years old. Bao was 77 years old. Duke Huan was 59 years old.

Led by Duke Huan of Qi, troops of Song and Cao helped save Xing, and defeated troops of Di.

In Autumn, Duke Min of Lu met Duke Huan of Qi to ally at place Luogu (maybe in today's Pinyin County or Boxing County, Shandong).

In winter, Zhong Sunqiu of Qi, went to State Lu to convey his sympathy; he said to Duke Huan of Qi, "Until Qingfu is done away with, the crisis in the State Lu will not be over."

简子生平传略图谱

管子生平传略图谱

王京龙／文
夏晓慧／译

公元前660年（辛酉），齐桓公二十六年

管仲76岁，鲍叔牙78岁，齐桓公60岁。

春，齐人迁阳（亦说灭阳，阳国故城在今山东省沂水县）。

夏，狄侵齐。

庆父出奔莒国，后畏罪自杀。鲁庆父之乱，齐高子将南阳之甲兵，立僖公而城鲁，以存鲁嗣。鲁人以为美谈，曰"犹望高子也"。

狄人灭亡卫国。卫国君寄住曹邑。齐桓公在管仲的建议下，派遣公子无亏率军助卫戍守。齐侯赠卫戴公乘马（四匹），祭服五称，牛、羊、豕、鸡、狗皆三百，与门材，赠卫文公夫人鱼轩，重锦三十匹。

660 BC (Xinyou Period), the 26th year of Duke Huan of Qi

Guan was 76 years old. Bao was 78 years old. Duke Huan was 60 years old.

In Spring, State Qi moved State Yang to another place. It was also said that State Yang was put out. This ancient city is in today's Yishui County, Shandong.

In Summer, minority Di invaded State Qi.

Qingfu of Lu run away to the State Ju and later killed himself to escape punishment. During the chaos of Qingfu's rebellions, Prince Gao of Qi led soldiers with armour from Nanyang, appointed Duke Xi and constructed a city for the people of Lu and their descendant. His deeds were passed on with approval among the people in Lu. People was saying, "How grateful Prince Gao was!"

Troops of minority Di had State Wei perished. The ruler of Wei lodged at a place in State Cao. With the proposal by Guan Zhong, Duke Huan had his prince Wukui leading an army stationed nearby, guarding the Wei. Duke Huan presented Duke Dai of Wei four saddle horses and vestments of five suits; livestock including cows, sheep, pigs, chickens, and dogs, each of 300; doors-making materials; and presented Duchess an elegant, wooden vehicle with top roof decorated with skin of fish, and brocade of about 1,000 meters.

公元前659年（壬戌），齐桓公二十七年

管仲77岁，鲍叔牙79岁，齐桓公61岁。

齐桓公取哀姜杀之，以尸归鲁。

狄人又侵略邢国，占领了邢国的都城。齐桓公和管仲率领齐、宋、曹三国军队救邢。齐桓公召集诸侯在夷仪（在今山东省聊城境）为邢国建筑了一座新城，作为邢国的国都。

郑亲齐，楚人伐郑，齐侯会鲁公、宋公、郑伯、曹伯、邾人谋救郑也。

659 BC (Renxu Period), the 27th year of Duke Huan of Qi

Guan was 77 years old. Bao was 79 years old. Duke Huan was 61 years old.

Duke Huan of Qi had Duchess Aijiang killed and returned her corpse to Lu. (She was licentious with a younger brother of Duke Zhuang.)

Minority Di invaded Xing again and occupied the capital. Led by Duke Huan and Guan Zhong, troops from three states, Qi, Song and Cao, helped save Xing. Duke Huan convened the feudal princes and had a new city built as the capital for Xing at Yiyi, in today's Liaocheng City, Shandong.

State Zheng had close relationship with Qi. So when Chu descended upon Zheng, Duke Huan met Duke of Lu, Duke of Song, Earl of Zheng, Earl of Cao and Ruler of Zhu to help save Zheng.

公元前658年（癸亥），齐桓公二十八年

管仲78岁，鲍叔牙80岁，齐桓公62岁。

卫文公有狄乱，告急于齐。齐桓公率诸侯师伐狄。又为卫国在楚丘（在今河南省滑县）建了一座新城，把暂住曹邑的卫君和他的人民迁到楚丘，以楚丘为新国都。

秋九月，齐桓公与宋（在今河南省商丘一带）、江（在今河南省息县西南）、黄（在今河南潢川县）三国之君盟于贯（在河南商丘西北，与山东曹县接界）。

658 BC (Guihai Period）, the 28th year of Duke Huan of Qi

Guan was 78 years old. Bao was 80 years old. Duke Huan was 62 years old.

Duke Wen of Wei had chaos with minority Di and asked for emergency help from Qi. The troops of the feudal princes, led by Duke Huan, dispatched an expedition against Di. Also, a new city was built for Wei at Chuqiu (in today's Huaxian County, Henan Province) to adjourn the ruler of Wei and his people temporarily.

In September, Duke Huan of Qi had a summit meeting with rulers of Song (in Shangqiu, Henan), Jiang (southwest of Xixian County, Henan) and Huang (Huangchuan County, Henan) at Guan (at the northwest of Shangqiu in Henan bordering Caoxian County in Shandong).

公元前657年（甲子），齐桓公二十九年

管仲79岁，鲍叔牙81岁，齐桓公63岁。

楚成王意欲和齐桓公争夺霸主的地位，就派军队进攻离它比较近的郑国。郑国向齐国求救。

秋，齐桓公会宋、江、黄三国于阳谷，谋伐楚。

冬，鲁公子季友如齐莅盟。

齐桓公与蔡姬乘舟于圃，荡公，公惧变色，禁之不可，公怒，归之，未绝之也，蔡人嫁之。

657 BC (Jiazi Period), the 29th year of Duke Huan of Qi

Guan was 79 years old. Bao was 81 years old. Duke Huan was 63 years old.

King Cheng of Chu was intending to compete with Duke Huan of Qi for the lord protector status and sent his troops invading Zheng, which was not far away. Zheng cried for help from Qi. In autumn, Duke Huan met with rulers of Song, Jiang and Huang at place Yanggu, seeking to descending upon Chu.

In winter, Prince Jiyou of Lu visited Qi to be present at the alliance ceremony.

Duke Huan and his wife Cai Ji strolled about, boating at a park. Cai Ji waggled the boat joking on purpose and Duke Huan was frightened but couldn't stop her. In a rage, he let Cai Ji go back to State Cai but didn't end their marriage. Her brother was not happy and had his sister Cai Ji remarried.

公元前656年（乙丑），齐桓公三十年

管仲80岁，鲍叔牙82岁，齐桓公64岁。

　　春，齐侯会鲁公、宋公、陈侯、卫侯、郑伯、许男、曹伯侵蔡，蔡溃，遂伐楚，次于陉（在今河南省沁阳境内）。夏，楚王使屈完将兵扞齐，齐师推次召陵，桓公矜屈完以其众。屈完曰："君以道则可，若不，则楚方城以为城，江汉以为沟，君安能进乎？"乃与屈完盟而去。秋，齐伐陈。齐桓公还师过陈，陈辕涛涂恶其过陈，诈齐出东道，桓公怒，执辕涛涂。冬，齐会鲁、宋、卫、郑、许、曹侵陈。陈成，归辕涛涂。

656 BC (Yichou Period), the 30th year of Duke Huan of Qi

Guan was 80 years old. Bao was 82 years old. Duke Huan was 64 years old.

In Spring, Duke Huan met Duke of Lu, Duke of Song, Marquis of Chen, Marquis of Wei, Earl of Zheng, Baron of Xu, Earl of Cao, invaded and made Cai badly defeated; then moving on to invade Chu, with all united troops stationed at Xing (in today's Qinyang, Henan Province). In summer, Ruler Cheng of Chu ordered his minister Qu Wan to defend united troops led by Qi. Then for the time being, united troops stationed at place Shaoling. Troops of several states drawn up in battle array, Duke Huan took Qu Wan with him in the same chariot to survey them. Qu Wan said, "If Your Lordship appease the people by your virtue, who will dare to refuse to submit you? But if you resort to force, the State Chu has the Hill of Fangcheng as a wall and the Han River for the city moat. Numerous as your forces are, they will not prevail." Alliance formed between Qu Wan on his lord behalf and Duke Huan of other states. Both troops left peacefully. In autumn, troops of Qi descended upon Chen. On their way back home, troops would pass through Chen. Yuan Taotu, a minister of Chen, was not happy with such arrangement and was tricking troops of Qi to go through east way instead. This made Duke Huan angry and he captured Yuan Taotu. In winter, troops from Qi, Lu, Song, Wei, Zheng, Xu and Cao invaded disloyal Chen. Without fighting, Chen asked for peace and Qi let go Chen's minister Yuan Taotu home.

公元前655年（丙寅），齐桓公三十一年

管仲81岁，鲍叔牙83岁，齐桓公65岁。

周王室内部发生王位之争。齐桓公为了保全太子郑的地位，联合八国诸侯在首止（今河南省淮阳东，卫地）与太子郑订盟，以确定周太子的地位。

655 BC (Bingyin Period）, the 31st year of Duke Huan of Qi

Guan was 81 years old. Bao was 83 years old. Duke Huan was 65 years old.

There was a chaos in fighting for the throne, within the palace of King of Western Zhou Dynasty. In order to preserve and confirm the heir status of Prince Zheng of Zhou Dynasty, Duke Huan united all other eight feudal princes and formed an alliance with prince Zheng at place Shouzhi, State Wei (in today's east of Huaiyang, Henan Province).

公元前654年（丁卯），齐桓公三十二年

管仲82岁，鲍叔牙84岁，齐桓公66岁。

夏，齐桓公因郑文公在首止不盟而逃会，遂率齐、鲁、宋、陈、卫、曹七国联军讨伐郑国，围郑之新城（今河南省密县之东南）。齐桓公对诸侯宣告郑文公之罪。秋，楚国围攻齐之盟国许国，意欲解救郑之危。齐桓公果然撤去围郑的诸侯联军，解救许国后还军。

654 BC (Dingmao Period）, the 32nd year of Duke Huan of Qi

Guan was 82 years old. Bao was 84 years old. Duke Huan was 66 years old.

In summer, because Duke Wen of Zheng evaded Shouzhi Alliance in supporting prince the heir Zheng, Duke Huan led united troops from other seven feudal princes to descend upon Zheng, by surrounding its capital, Xincheng (in today's southwest of Mixian County, Henan Province). Duke Huan declared the wrongdoings of Duke Wen. In Autumn, Chu sent its troops to siege Xu, an ally of Qi, in order to rescue the danger of Zheng. Duke Huan had to withdraw all united troops surrounding Zheng's capital and went back after saving the Xu.

公元前653年（戊辰），齐桓公三十三年

管仲83岁，鲍叔牙85岁，齐桓公67岁。

春，齐国再出兵讨伐郑国。

夏，郑国杀死从楚国叛逃投郑的申侯以取悦齐国，并向诸侯求和。

秋，齐桓公邀请鲁僖公、宋桓公、陈世子款、郑世子华在宁母（今山东省鱼台境）相会。

周惠王死，太子郑秘不发丧，先告难于齐国，请助其确立王位。

653 BC (Wuchen Period), the 33rd year of Duke Huan of Qi

Guan was 83 years old. Bao was 85 years old. Duke Huan was 67 years old.

In Spring, troops of Qi suppressed State Zheng again.

In summer, Zheng had Marquis of Shen, defecting from Chu, killed to please Qi, and asking for peace to all feudal princes.

In autumn, Duke Huan invited Duke Xi of Lu, Duke Huan of Song, Kuan the heir of Chen, Hua the heir of Zheng to meet at Ningmu (in today's Yutai, Shandong).

When King Hui of Western Zhou Dynasty passed away, his prince, the heir Zheng, didn't send out his obituary, but informed Qi first instead, asking support of the establishment of his throne status.

公元前652年（己巳），齐桓公三十四年

管仲84岁，鲍叔牙86岁，齐桓公68岁。

正月，齐桓公邀请鲁、宋、卫、许、曹等国国君和陈世子，与周襄王派出的大夫在洮（在山东省鄄城西南）订盟。郑文公因是重新服齐，请求加盟。齐桓公率各国诸侯确认太子郑的王位。于是周襄王讣告天下，为周惠王发丧。

652 BC (Jisi Period), the 34th year of Duke Huan of Qi

Guan was 84 years old. Bao was 86 years old. Duke Huan was 68 years old.

In January, Duke Huan invited rulers from Lu, Song, Wei, Xu and Cao, also the Heir of Chen, and a minister sent by King Xiang of Western Zhou Dynasty and formed an alliance at place Tao (in the southwest of Juan County, Shandong Province). Duke Wen of Zheng thus got convinced and asking to join the alliance. Duke Huan and all feudal princes confirmed the throne status of prince the heir Zheng. After that, King Xiang of Zhou announced the death of King Hui publicly, buried him accordingly at last.

公元前651年（庚午），齐桓公三十五年

管仲85岁，鲍叔牙87岁，齐桓公69岁。

夏，会诸侯于葵丘。这是齐桓公霸业顶峰的标志。

齐桓公与管仲请宋襄公做太子雍的外辅。太子雍是桓公夫人宋华子所生，故请宋襄公为外辅。

齐桓公葵丘会盟之后，意欲封禅，管仲劝止。

651 BC (Gengwu Period), the 35th year of Duke Huan of Qi

Guan was 85 years old. Bao was 87 years old. Duke Huan was 69 years old.

In summer, Duke Huan met and allied with the feudal princes at Kuiqiu. This summit meeting was the top notch of his accomplishments of obtaining the

管子生平系年　郭振华／绘

lord protector.

Duke Huan and Guan Zhong invited Duke Xiang of Song to tutor his prince Yong, as a foreign helper. Prince Yong was born by Song Huazi, Duke Huan's wife whose home was Song.

After the Kuiqiu Alliance, Duke Huan was intending to offer sacrifices to heaven at Mount Taishan. This kind of ceremony was conducted only by emperors formally. Guan Zhong disadvised.

公元前650年（辛未），齐桓公三十六年
管仲86岁，鲍叔牙88岁，齐桓公70岁。
夏，齐、许联合伐北戎。
王子党会齐国隰朋立姬夷吾为晋后。

650 BC (Xinwei Period), the 36th year of Duke Huan of Qi
Guan was 86 years old. Bao was 88 years old. Duke Huan was 70 years old.
In summer, Qi and Xu united to descended upon North Rong.
Minister Viscount Dang of King Zhou met minister Xi Peng of Qi. They appointed Ji Yiwu the queen of State Jin.

公元前649年（壬申），齐桓公三十七年
管仲87岁，鲍叔牙89岁，齐桓公71岁。
周襄王之弟叔带与戎、翟共谋伐周襄王，襄王欲诛叔带，叔带奔齐。

649 BC (Renshen Period), the 37th year of Duke Huan of Qi
Guan was 87 years old. Bao was 89 years old. Duke Huan was 71 years old.
Shudai, a half brother of King Xiang of Western Zhou Dynasty, conspired secretly with States Rong and Zhai to descended upon King Xiang; so King Xiang wanted to kill, Shudai, who had to escape quickly to Qi.

公元前648年（癸酉），齐桓公三十八年

管仲88岁，鲍叔牙90岁，齐桓公72岁。

冬，齐桓公派管仲、隰朋分赴周、晋调和。周襄王欲以上卿之礼对待管仲，管仲卒以下卿之礼而还礼。

648 BC (Guiyou Period), the 38th year of Duke Huan of Qi

Guan was 88 years old. Bao was 90 years old. Duke Huan was 72 years old.

In winter, Duke Huan sent Guan Zhong and Xi Peng to King Xiang of Western Zhou Dynasty and State Jin respectively to reconcile contradiction between Zhou and Jin. King Xiang of Western Zhou intended to treat Guan Zhong as official with a higher rank; Guan Zhong returned a salute still as a junior minister.

公元前647年（甲戌），齐桓公三十九年

管仲89岁，鲍叔牙91岁，齐桓公73岁。

周襄王弟带来奔齐。

夏，齐桓公邀请宋、鲁、陈、卫、郑、许、曹等国国君会于咸（今河南省濮县东南），谋戍周迁杞之策。

管仲有病，桓公往问后事，管仲荐隰朋。

647 BC (Jiaxu Period), the 39th year of Duke Huan of State Qi

Guan was 89 years old. Bao was 91 years old. Duke Huan was 73 years old.

Shudai, a half brother of King Xiang of Western Zhou, came to Qi for shelter.

In summer, Duke Huan of Qi invited rulers of Song, Lu, Chen, Wei, Zheng, Xu and Cao to meet at Xian (in today's southeast of Puxian County, Henan), planning to search a way to defend Western Zhou Dynasty and move tributary Qi (杞) to a safer place.

郭振华\绘

When Guan Zhong was seriously ill, Duke Huan payed a visit, inquiring what to do afterwards, thus minister Xi Peng was recommended to take his post.

公元前646年（乙亥），齐桓公四十年

管仲90岁，鲍叔牙92岁，齐桓公74岁。

春，齐桓公迁杞于缘陵，发动诸侯为杞筑城，给兵车百乘，士卒千人戍守。齐桓公问于宁戚曰："管子今年老矣，为弃寡人而就世也，吾恐法令不行，人多失职，百姓积怨，国多盗贼，吾何如而使奸邪不起，民足衣食乎？"宁戚对曰："要在得贤而任之。"

646 BC (Yihai Period), the 40th year of Duke Huan of Qi

Guan was 90 years old. Bao was 92 years old. Duke Huan was 74 years old.

In Spring, Duke Huan, together with the efforts of other feudal princes, had tributary Qi (杞) moved to Yuanling, with 100 chariots and 1,000 soldiers garrison. Duke Huan inquired Ning Qi, "Guan Zhong is old and has his days numbered. I am worrying that decree will not be effectively carried out. Officers will not do their duty well and people will not satisfy, as more robbery here and there. What is the best policy to keep the order and let people have enough food and cloth?" Ning replied, "A key point is to have those talented people in charge of state affairs."

公元前645年（丙子），齐桓公四十一年

管仲91岁，鲍叔牙93岁，齐桓公75岁。

春正月，鲁僖公朝齐，同于事天子之礼。三月，齐侯、鲁侯、宋公、陈侯、卫侯、郑伯、许男、曹伯盟于牡丘（在今山东省茌平东）。

鲍叔牙死，管仲举上衽而哭之，泣下如雨。

管仲死，桓公尽逐竖刁、易牙、开方等，食不甘，宫不治，苛病起，朝不肃。重新召回竖刁、易牙、开方等人。

645 BC (Bingzi Period), the 41st year of Duke Huan of Qi

Guan was 91 years old. Bao was 93 years old. Duke Huan was 75 years old.

In Spring, Duke Xi of Lu came visiting State Qi, but in the same rites as to be in front of the Son of Heaven. In March, Marquis of Qi, Marquis of Lu, Duke of Song, Marquis of Chen, Marquis of Wei, Baron of Xu and Earl of Cao got allied at Muqiu (in today's east of Chiping, Shandong).

When Bao Shuya died, Guan Zhong cried, burying his face with his gown high, shed running tears.

After Guan Zhong died, as advised, Duke Huan banished those 4 flattery courtiers from his palace, Shu Diao, Yi Ya, Kai Fang, etc; without those flattery courtiers around, Duke Huan lost his appetite and mind, and the harem and court were in disorder, his old illness occurred again, but no duty work on palace as usual. So Duke Huan recalled them back into his palace.

公元前644年（丁丑），齐桓公四十二年

齐桓公75岁。

戎伐周，周告急于齐，齐令诸侯各发卒戍周。

晋国公子重耳来齐，齐桓公妻之。

管仲死后十个月，隰朋卒。

淮夷逼迫鄫国（在今山东省苍山境内），齐桓公会和鲁、宋、陈、卫、郑、许、邢、曹等，为鄫国筑城。

644 BC (Dingchou Period), the 42nd year of Duke Huan of Qi

Duke Huan was 75 years old.

When minority Rong invaded Western Zhou Dynasty, so Zhou asked Qi for protect urgently; so Duke Huan ordered all feudal princes to send their troops to garrison.

Chong'er, a prince of State Jin came to Qi for help. Duke Huan had him married a girl of his family clan.

Ten months after Guan Zhong's death, Xi Peng died.

State Ceng (in today's Cangshan, Shandong) was coerced by Huaiyi, a tribe near the Huaihe River. Duke Huan, together with rulers of Lu, Song, Chern, Wei, Zheng, Xu, Xing and Cao, had a new capital built for Ceng.

公元前643年（戊寅），齐桓公四十三年

齐桓公76岁。

鲁灭项（在今河南省项城境内），齐桓公扣留了鲁僖公。后齐灭项。

竖刁、易牙、开方等近侍与桓公公子作乱。桓公卒。尸停床上六十七日，虫出于户。十二月乙亥（初八）日，公子无诡立，辛巳（十五）日夜，敛殡。据考，齐桓公死于公元前643年9月12日。

643 BC (Wuyin Period), the 43rd year of Duke Huan of Qi

Duke Huan was 76 years old.

State Lu put out the State Xiang (in today's Xiangcheng, Henan Province). Duke Huan of Qi had Duke Xi of Lu withheld. Later State Qi had the State Xiang put out.

Courtiers of Duke Huan, Shu Diao, Yi Ya, and Kai Fang made troubles in the palace. All five princes of Duke Huan fighting for the throne. When Duke Huan passed away, his corpse was on bed for 67 days long, decomposed, even with worms coming out through the windows. On December 8th, his prince Wugui was on the enthronement and finally on 15th night, Duke Huan was put formally in the coffin. According to studies, Duke Huan died on September 12th, 643 BC.

简子生平传略图谱

管子生平传略图谱

王京龙／文

夏晓慧／译

后 记

让一个与齐文化研究不沾边的门外汉，来为这本专业性极强的专著写后记，可谓前所未闻……但这样的事偏偏就让我一个年逾古稀的老者摊上了，所以真是左右为难，不敢应承……

《管子生平传略图谱》的课题申请立项人、文稿主笔王京龙教授的夫人宁秀红先生再次找到我："郭老师，你们这些年他写您画，好不容易得来的辛勤成果有个圆满，眼看书就要交出版社了，人却先走了。若不是齐文化研究院领导、老师们千方百计地支持并积极联系，怎么会有这本书的顺利出版？毕竟有些感激的话还得有个地方、有个知情人替京龙去说……"

王京龙教授的突然病逝，使正处于完善中的《管子生平传略图谱》书稿一下陷入尴尬的境地，书的目录、作者简介、后记等一些细节的内容，都需要有人来一一补齐。作为此书的合著者之一，我此时只有努力承担起京龙先生未完成的这些事，确属责无旁贷了。

2016年，根据省委宣传部"关于推进齐鲁优秀传统文化传承创新工程重点项目的通知"精神，山东理工大学齐文化研究院和山东省齐文化研究基地以其在研项目为基础，经省高工委同意，申报了由山东省齐文化研究基地首席专家王京龙教授主持的两个项目，一个是"研究阐发"型的《管子通论》，一个是"普及教育"型的《管子生平传略图谱》。当时学校已将这两个项目，作为培育项目，拨款启动在研。

鉴于我曾为京龙教授所著《管子与孔子的历史对话》（插图本）画过插图，反响还不错，所以这次京龙便又找我合作。我与京龙是君子之交，义不容辞，自然也就答应了下来。他告诉我这次要画四十幅，不叫插图，美其名曰"圣迹图"，即书与画的内容在结构上是一个相对独立的系统。画虽以书为据，同样可构架一个相对完整的说明系统。所以，这本书就整体而言，不看书面文章就是一册画，不看画就是一册书。文字简单，图画简洁，书与画合而一体。相信选用这种形式全面阐释管子的思想以及其辅佐齐桓公首霸春秋的成功实践，不仅是件很新鲜、很有意思的事，也许还会有一定的价值。

谁料想，申报后《管子通论》很快获准立项，而《管子生平传略图谱》却迟迟没有接到立项通知。虽然没有收到立项通知，但考虑到项目本身的价值和意义以及已经启动的实际情况，王教授在征询有关专家意见的基础上，仍然在按照项目要求正常研究的同时，对原来的设计方案做了较大改动。而且这次的文稿增加了英文翻译，力求提升管子生平轨迹在国际上的传播能力和空间。

2018年底，由王京龙教授著文、夏晓慧老师译（英）文和我负责绘制的书稿全部完成，最后由王京龙教授统编定稿。王京龙教授高兴地说："山东乃'齐鲁之邦'，齐有管子，鲁有孔子。他们作为中国传统文化中的典型代表，对国家和民族发展的优势支撑自然不言而喻。管子死后近百年，孔子才出生，但后来的孔子看到了管子的伟大。管子是齐文化的星标，无管子则无言及齐文化。"管子和孔子同处春秋，管子是齐文化崛起的人文巨峰；孔子是鲁文化崛起的人文巨峰。鲁有《孔子圣迹图》，齐也应有《管子生平传略图谱》，我们期望把管子的功业和思想简要而形象的展现于世，现在就差一步（出版）之遥了。

本书的出版承蒙山东省政协原副主席、齐鲁文化研究基地首席专家、山东理工大学齐文化研究院院长王志民先生在学术上的始终支持，他还在事务繁忙的情况下欣然为本书撰写序文；山东理工大学齐文化研究院张灿贤教授为本课题的立项及京龙先生逝后该研究成果的顺利出版做了不少工作；院办公室贺玲主任也以同样的热情给予了大量帮助：此实感人至深者，特别在此深致谢意。

管子生平传略图谱

王京龙／文
夏晓慧／译

当这件我们想要做、必须做，费尽周折、竭尽全力去做的极有意义的事，终于收到同意"接受出版"的消息时，我们的心里不禁生出一种从未有过的责任感和使命感。我想，这是我们三位合作者的初衷，是齐文化研究院领导和为本书的出版付出辛劳的中国海洋大学出版社编辑老师们的初衷，也是所有支持、帮助我们为该书的顺利出版而付出智慧和心血的同仁及朋友们的初衷吧。

郭振华于舍下

2020年5月1日

後記

后记

郭振华／绘

POSTSCRIPT

As a starter, I never thought that one day there would be a chance for me, an old man in his 70s, and a layman of Kingdom Qi's Culture study, to write a postscript for such a professional work. I was in a dilemma and reluctant to accept doing it, as I was not sure if I would express and explain the intention envisioned by its initiator; and even if there is a slightest difference to him, that would be the last thing I wished.

Initiator professor Wang Jinglong is the manuscript chief writer and the project applicant of *Master Guan Zhong's Lifetime Pictures Story*. His sudden death of illness made all related work run into a pause and chaotic. His unfinished work faced an awkwardness: its book contents, introduction postscript... needed to be worked out to make it complete. As his partner, I once made my drawings as illustration based on his manuscript. Now facing this unfinished work left by, the only choice for me is to bear the work and do it well.

So the other day, Madam Ning Xiuhong, his wife, came to visit me again, saying, "Professor Guo, I appreciate your hard work and cooperation over the years, by drawing illustrations based on his manuscript. Finally it is going to be a perfect ending after time-consuming and painstaking, on the horizon to have it published. And without the support from leading body of Kingdom Qi's Culture Academy (KQCA) or the sustaining support from those colleagues and friends, how can we have it published successfully? After all, a gratitude and appreciation has to be expressed, on behalf of my husband Jinglong." I can do nothing but accepting her invitation then.

In 2016, according to the policy from the Propaganda Department of the CPC Shandong Provincial Committee, on notification of propelling key projects on traditional culture inheritance and innovation, KQCA of Shandong University of Technology (SDUT) and Shandong Provincial Research Base on Kingdom Qi's Culture (PBKQC), co-applied two projects, with professor Wang Jinglong presiding, chief expert on PBKQC, namely the academic *The General Theory of Master Guan Zhong* and the popular *Master Guan Zhong's Lifetime Pictures Story*. These two projects, as cultivating projects, had already been run with allocating fund from SDUT. The two projects were based on ongoing projects, with the approval from Shandong Provincial Higher Education Working Committee.

As we two once cooperated on *A Historical Dialogue between Master Guan Zhong and Confucius* (Qilu Press) with a good response, Mr.Wang Jinglong came to visit me, proposing a second time cooperation. With gentleman's friendship for years, I accepted at once. He outlined in detail that there would be 40 related drawings which are more than illustrations. We called it sage's footprints; in other words, manuscript and related drawing stand alone, and drawings are based on the manuscript. The drawings, comparatively speaking, frame a complete system, without reading its words description. It would be a book if you just read all the manuscript instead of its drawings. Simplified words and concise drawings formed an organic one. We firmly believe that it would be unique in style and interesting, and would be likely in value for study as well.

Unexpectedly, after the application, the academic project *General Theory of Master Guan Zhong* was approved soon; while the popular project *Master Guan Zhong's Lifetime Pictures Story* took a long time waiting for the approval. During this time, taking into consideration of its research value and its startup, after consulting related experts, its research work was under way as normal.

後記

后记

郭振华／绘

Initiator Wang made a big modification by adding an English version, making it bilingual, in order to promote Master Guan Zhong's influence to international readers.

At the end of 2018, a complete draft, with Mr. Wang as the chief manuscript writer, Xia Xiaohui as the translator for the English version, and me for the drawings, was ready in hand and it was edited and finalized by Professor Wang himself. Joyfully he said, "Shandong is a place originated from ancient Kingdoms Qi and Lu. In Kingdom Lu there was sage Confucius, while in Kingdom Qi there was Master Guan Zhong. Both of them are everlasting representatives of Chinese traditional culture. Their brand value and superiority is of utmost importance to China and Chinese culture. Confucius was born almost one hundred years later after Master Guan Zhong passed away, but he read out the importance of Master Guan Zhong. Master Guan was the asterisk of Kingdom Qi's Culture. There would be no right to mention Kingdom Qi's Culture without Guan Zhong. Both of them were from the Spring and Autumn Period. Confucius was a representative of Kingdom Lu's Culture, whereas Master Guan Zhong was a representative of Kingdom Qi's Culture. As there was a book called *Confucius Footprint Story*, there must be another book called *Master Guan Zhong's Lifetime Pictures Story*. Briefly and visually showing Master Guan Zhong's outstanding achievements and great thinking to the world is our long time expectation. Now the final publication is on the horizon."

The publication of this book is a collaborative effort that has been built upon the contributions of many great people:

Mr. Wang Zhimin, dean of KQCA under SDUT, chief expert of Culture Research Base of Kingdoms Qi and Lu, former vice-chairman of CPPCC Shandong Province, provided constant academic assitance and joyfully wrote this preface despite his busy duty affair and academic research.

Professor Zhang Canxian from KQCA under SDUT, did a lot of work for the project approval, its research output evaluation and successful publication, particularly after Mr. Wang's pass-away;

He Ling, a KQCA office director, also shared her warm attention during this whole work.

Also thanks to those editors from China Ocean University Press and all those colleague and friends. It is hard for me to make a long list of those who showed their support, wisdom and effort for the smooth publication of this book.

And most importantly, when there is a chance in your life time that you can do something of significant value, of what you desire and what you must, do your best. The book *Master Guan Zhong's Lifetime Pictures Story* is just such interesting and worth-doing; when the final green light on "publishing acceptance" came, we cannot help having a sense of duty and mission. I firmly believe this is the initial intention of we three partners and is also shared by all above. And being an offspring of Chinese nationality, each of us is committed and duty bound to do one's mission well, in any case.

Guo Zhenhua at home

May 1st, 2020

後記

后记

郭振华／绘